"I'm a huge Stephen Mansfield fan. His latest book, *Ask the Question*, stresses our need to better understand what our candidates believe about religion. We need a more sophisticated level of discussion about the faith of our candidates. You need to read this book now!"

**Pat Williams**
Senior Vice President, Orlando Magic

"Stephen Mansfield's latest book, *Ask the Question*, takes on one of the most common points of contention in the news today: religion. He's demanding that candidates come clean on their beliefs before they get to the Oval Office. He's right, and he makes his case in a unique, fascinating manner that is rich in American history."

**Brian Kilmeade**
*FOX News*

"There's no such thing as private religion, and Stephen Mansfield understands as few others do that all real faith is public. So shouldn't we know what our prospective leaders believe? As Mansfield demonstrates, we cannot afford not to."

**Joel J. Miller**
author, *The Revolutionary Paul Revere*

"Stephen Mansfield has done it again! *Ask the Question* will challenge you, make you think, and provide incredible insights. You may have been afraid to 'ask the question' before. No more. You'll ask it and with the purpose of understanding, voting properly, and acting responsibly!"

**Steve Brown**
professor/broadcaster

"In *Ask the Question*, Stephen Mansfield helps us understand the role of faith in the lives of our presidents. His approach is neither partisan nor partial to a particular aspect of religion. This book helps us educate ourselves about how religion shapes the decision-making of our leaders. Stephen Mansfield challenges both voters and the media to ask the right questions."

**Dr. Joel C. Hunter**
Senior Pastor, Northland Church

"Both Republican and Democrat presidential candidates have hoodwinked people of faith for years. The truth is that all candidates, whether secular or religious, hold certain beliefs, certain values, that will shape what they do when they get into office. Stephen Mansfield is right. We need to ask candidates what those beliefs are. This need is more urgent now than ever."

**J. C. Watts Jr.**
former US congressman, Oklahoma

"Nothing has impacted my personal value system more than my faith, and that's the way it should be. So much of who we are is wrapped up in what we believe. That's why it blows my mind that we aren't 'allowed' to dig in and have a good discussion about our political candidates' core spiritual beliefs. In *Ask the Question*, my friend Stephen Mansfield has the courage to hit this issue head-on and call for a higher level of discussion around faith and politics. Every voter in the country should read this book!"

**Dave Ramsey**
*New York Times* bestselling author;
nationally syndicated radio show host

"There is a reason Stephen Mansfield's books—*The Faith of George W. Bush*, *The Faith of Barack Obama*, and *Lincoln's Battle with God*—are so wildly popular. We know that what our politicians believe affects how they will govern. This book gives us a chance to see the impact of faith on those who hold the highest office in the land."

**Todd Lake**
Vice President for Spiritual Development,
Belmont University

"In *Ask the Question*, Stephen Mansfield makes a persuasive case for why it's both important and appropriate to expect candidates for president of the United States to be open and detailed about their personal religious journeys and beliefs. This is especially important in an era when religious beliefs are becoming more and more personalized and eclectic and it's not very clear how those personal expressions of faith would impact or shape a political leader's worldview and decision-making process. I would recommend this book to anyone who is interested in the intersection of personal faith and public service, faith and politics."

**Jim Wallis**
President, Sojourners;
Editor in Chief, *Sojourners* magazine

# ASK THE QUESTION

## Also by Stephen Mansfield

*The Character and Greatness of Winston Churchill:*
*Hero in Time of Crisis*

*Then Darkness Fled: The Liberating Wisdom of Booker T. Washington*

*Forgotten Founding Father: The Heroic Legacy of George Whitefield*

*The Faith of George W. Bush*

*The Faith of the American Soldier*

*Benedict XVI: His Life and Mission*

*The Faith of Barack Obama*

*The Search for God and Guinness*

*Lincoln's Battle with God*

*Killing Jesus*

*Mansfield's Book of Manly Men*

*The Miracle of the Kurds*

# ASK THE
# QUESTION

★　★　★　★　★

## WHY WE MUST DEMAND RELIGIOUS CLARITY
## FROM OUR PRESIDENTIAL CANDIDATES

## STEPHEN MANSFIELD

**BakerBooks**
*a division of Baker Publishing Group*
Grand Rapids, Michigan

Published by Baker Books
a division of Baker Publishing Group
P.O. Box 6287, Grand Rapids, MI 49516-6287
www.bakerbooks.com

Printed in the United States of America

Library of Congress Cataloging-in-Publication Data is on file at the Library of Congress, Washington, DC.

ISBN 978-0-8010-1887-9

Scripture quotations labeled KJV are from the King James Version of the Bible.

Scripture quotations labeled NIV are from the Holy Bible, New International Version®. NIV®. Copyright © 1973, 1978, 1984, 2011 by Biblica, Inc.™ Used by permission of Zondervan. All rights reserved worldwide. www.zondervan.com

16   17   18   19   20   21   22        7   6   5   4   3   2

To

JOHN SEIGENTHALER SR.,
*friend and inspiration*

# Contents

# Contents

In religion and politics people's beliefs and convictions are in almost every case gotten at second-hand, and without examination, from authorities who have not themselves examined the questions at issue but have taken them at second-hand from other non-examiners, whose opinions about them were not worth a brass farthing.

Mark Twain

# Foreword

by David Aikman

The year was 1976, and *Newsweek* magazine had declared it "The Year of the Evangelical." Pollster George Gallup had estimated that the number of Americans who considered themselves "evangelical" might be as high as fifty million. The greatest political event of that year was the emergence of former Georgia governor Jimmy Carter as the Democratic presidential candidate. Carter had declared himself a Christian early in his political campaign, and he had made it clear that he was of the "born-again" variety.

As one of the only two born-again Christian reporters at the news organization where I worked, I was tickled with amusement at the groans both in print and in ordinary conversation from seasoned Washington journalists who simply hadn't a clue what Jimmy Carter was talking about. The phone lines between Washington, DC, and parts of rural Kansas or the Bible Belt were soon buzzing, with reporters asking their back-home "religious" relatives what being "born again" meant. It was a classic example of journalistic ignorance generated by a lack of education and a lack even of interest in a phenomenon that was at the time ricocheting through the

United States. You really had to be intentionally neglectful of the American cultural scene to miss the fact that the United States was going through a surging evangelical revival in the late 1970s.

Unfortunately, the same provincialism about religious faith sprung up in a much more dangerous environment when the exiled Ayatollah Khomeini returned in triumph to Iran in early 1979. He was welcomed by crowds in the hundreds of thousands and quickly established a hard-line Shiite Islamic regime that overcame all democratic and secular resistance. Americans learned painfully how new and unexpected the environment of Iran had become when in November 1979 the United States Embassy in Tehran was taken over by radical protesters and fifty-two American diplomats were held hostage for 444 days.

Anyone who had taken seriously the pronouncements of the Iranian leader Khomeini when he was still in exile in Iraq and France would not have been surprised at all that he was going to establish a tyrannical dictatorship. Nevertheless, that did not prevent senior American diplomats and experienced journalists from uttering the idiotic comment that Khomeini was some sort of "saint." I recall a strenuous argument with a fellow writer at the magazine where I worked. She insisted—purely on the basis that, as an opponent of the Shah, who had made some serious Islamic religious pronouncements—he was a sort of Gandhi-like figure. That, in my view, was tantamount to how out of touch an American would have been in the 1930s if he had declared Adolf Hitler to be a European mystic because he talked a lot about "Providence" and had not officially renounced his birth religion of Roman Catholicism.

Stephen Mansfield is certainly correct that most Americans today, particularly in the political arena, subscribe to a smorgasbord of beliefs that together constitute their personal worldview. The actual word *worldview* is not one generally used by most journalists or academics, probably because they don't acknowledge that their own perception of the reality on which they are reporting was acquired

14

during their education and subsequent journalistic experience. A failure to acknowledge that you yourself have a worldview makes it extremely difficult to assess what the worldview might be of campaigning political leaders. Indeed, ignorance of one's own galaxy of perceptions makes it all but impossible even to pose sensible and astute questions to any person or political figure about what that person believes.

One of the most interesting examples in my experience of the lack of awareness of a worldview and therefore the lack of ability to perceive the worldview of others occurred during the collapse of communism in Eastern Europe in the year 1989. Most of my journalistic colleagues believed that communism was being run out of town because it had failed to deliver economically. But I had met with many Czechoslovak dissidents long before they were in a position to take over the government of the country. They all had made it clear that their objection to the system had nothing to do with its economic performance and everything to do with the way it controlled every area of human life. One of the great "aha! moments" in my own reporting career was hearing the Czechoslovak dissident Václav Havel explain to an audience of several thousand people assembled in Prague, the capital of Czechoslovakia, that the issue of the revolt against the regime was really an issue of the country rejoining the mainstream of European history. The poor economic performance of communism was only a minute part of the collapse of the system throughout Eastern Europe. The Czechoslovak protest against communism was a moral revolt before it became a politically effective revolt.

As a reporter in Washington throughout much of the decade of the 1980s, I was always surprised by how little attention was given by reporters to the actual beliefs of the politicians and leaders on whom they were reporting. The early 1980s found most otherwise skeptical Americans almost sophomoric in their optimism about

China's future political development. Thus, when the Tiananmen Square student protests got on the way in April 1989, there was a widespread reluctance to believe that the regime might be willing to crush it with great violence. The assumption was that since China's leader Deng Xiaoping had visited the United States at the beginning of the decade and had donned a cowboy hat, he wasn't really a serious communist. Yet anybody who knew anything about Deng's career knew that he not only was a serious communist but also had used violence at various times on his upward political pathway to crush opposition to the communist regime in China. How did anyone know that Deng was a serious communist? By reading what he had written about his own beliefs.

I came to the conclusion that deep philosophical beliefs about anything had been marginalized in the minds of reporters because in most cases they lacked any conscious philosophical or faith beliefs of their own and had been educated to believe that religious faith was always a private issue, was probably a historical relic, and had nothing to do with real life or the policies that elected or unelected leaders might actually implement once they were in power.

There is, of course, another factor in the reluctance of reporters to ask profound questions about the beliefs of the people on whom they are reporting. There exists a completely false assumption among some reporters that if you ask what a person believes about religion, you are violating the constitutional line of the separation of church and state. That is tantamount to refusing to pose a question to an aspiring physicist about whether or not he or she believes the world to be flat.

It is entirely fair to ask of any person, whether or not he or she is aspiring to political power, what he or she believes about life in general and about particular expressions of human culture and politics. What the person asking the question then has to do is be truthful and accurate in writing down the answer. There is a natural human tendency to report inaccurately on beliefs we do not agree with. But the public can only benefit from the asking of important questions about faith if the answer is accurately reported. The pronounced secular tilt of cultural elites throughout the West in general and in the United States in particular makes them very reluctant to acknowledge any worldview or attitude with which they do not personally have sympathy. This was surely one factor in the gross misjudgment of the Iranian regime by Americans who saw it taking form before their very eyes. Indeed, a failure to take seriously the beliefs of others surely had a lot to do with the failure of the United States to anticipate the events of September 11, 2001, and, after they happened, to account for them.

There is now a greater need than ever for aspiring political leaders to be honest and truthful about what they believe. But there is a concomitant need for reporters or observers of the comments they make to be fair, accurate, and truthful in making those opinions known to the larger public. A common Latin rubric that is well known in American life is *caveat emptor*—"let the buyer beware." A consumer of news reports or broadcasts should surely adopt a similar motto: *caveat lector*—"let the reader [or viewer] beware." After all, "What do you believe?" is something that posers of the question of faith to others should be willing to ask of themselves. Truthfulness and fairness, after all, ought to be the common coin of all communication among people.

David Aikman<br>
Oxford University<br>
Former Senior Correspondent and Station Chief, *Time* magazine

# Prologue

> The problem with writing about religion is that you run the risk of offending sincerely religious people, and then they come after you with machetes.
>
> Dave Barry

It is Saturday, April 25, 2015, and the White House Correspondents' Association Dinner is just beginning. Most of the twenty-six hundred guests have arrived, the more famous and fashionably attired having strolled a press-lined red carpet as they entered the stylish Washington Hilton. The president and first lady have been seated, along with the other luminaries, at the head table. All have been publicly introduced. Scholarships and awards have been announced. Now Christi Parsons, the association's president, is concluding her remarks. The 101st occasion of this capital city tradition is well underway.

There is a hint of sadness this evening. Earlier today a massive earthquake struck Katmandu in Nepal. It killed thousands, made tens of thousands homeless, and caused an avalanche on Mount Everest that crushed nineteen people to death. Four of them were Americans, including Dan Fredinburg, a Google executive. Many here knew him. Some of the news anchors at the dinner were on the air all day giving updates and recountings for viewers just tuning in. The earthquake had been much discussed over cocktails earlier this evening.

Still, it is the glitziest night of the year on the Washington social calendar, and spirits are rising. This event has been called the "Nerds Prom." Tonight it seems the cool kids have decided to invade. Appearing with nearly every news anchor and reporter in the city, as well as with the network executives who keep them in check, are the dazzling stars of sport, stage, and screen. Some news veterans have been heard to complain that the dinner is no longer about the correspondents and their networks. Now it is all about the parent companies that own them and who crassly invite the famous as part of building a brand. It means that for one evening a year, Washington, DC, turns into Hollywood West. Tonight, judging by the number of selfies newsmen are taking with starlets, the nerds don't seem to mind the change.

All the network news royalty are here, of course, but so are Bradley Cooper, Lucy Liu, Jane Seymour, Alfre Woodard, Jane Fonda, and *Sports Illustrated* swimsuit issue cover model Hannah Davis. Connie Britton, producer and star of the TV show *Nashville*, seems in constant need of help with the train of her dress. Kardashians and Trumps are ever present. Bill Belichick, coach of the New England Patriots, is here, and so is Seattle Seahawks quarterback Russell Wilson, who brought his grandmother with him. An actor from the HBO series *Game of Thrones* is seated, as is singing star John Legend, who can't stop snapping iPhone photos of his supermodel wife, Chrissy Teigen. Executives at ABC shocked everyone by bringing the entire cast of their hit TV comedy *Modern Family*.

It is an evening of stunning glamour—a boozy, raucous, self-conscious occasion of cavernous cleavage and sparkling dresses stretched tightly over unavoidable derrieres. There are tuxedoed men with oversized heads and famous people trying not to embarrass themselves by fawning over those more famous still. It is a night to see and be seen, a night to be remembered. After appetizers of jumbo lump crabmeat with jicama have been served, mango pepitas and baby oak salad, smoked paprika rubbed filet, foraged wild mushroom ragout, and mascarpone cheese stone grits will be served with a Chateau Ste. Michelle and a Simi Cabernet Sauvignon.

Cecily Strong of *Saturday Night Live* is the celebrity host. She is now bringing the edgy humor all expect. "Let's give it up for the Secret Service," she has just said. "They're the only law enforcement agency in the nation that will get in trouble if a black man gets shot." This is her tone all night. She started with, "The Washington Hilton, you guys! If these walls could talk, they'd probably say, 'Clean me.'"

The president spoke just before her. He took the traditional jabs: "Just this week Michele Bachmann predicted I would bring about the biblical end of days. Now, that's a legacy! That's big! I mean, Lincoln, Washington, they didn't do that!" He was also, as expected, self-deprecating: "Six years into my presidency people still say I'm arrogant. Aloof. Condescending. People are so dumb. That's why I don't meet with them."

Midway into his speech Mr. Obama was joined by comedian Keegan-Michael Key, who played his "anger translator." When the president assured, "Despite our differences we count on the press to shed light," his anger translator continued, "And we can count on *FOX News* to terrify all white people with some nonsense!" And so it went.

It has all been memorable. Now it is over. Guests say their good-byes and rush to limousines. Some call Uber. The after-parties await. The hottest ticket this year is the Vanity Fair/Bloomberg Party at the French ambassador's residence in Sheridan-Kalorama. It will go all night. Those not invited will be glued to Instagram tomorrow to see photos of Chrissy Teigen's legs and confirmation that Bradley Cooper was indeed flirting with Nancy Pelosi.

It is the great night of the year, a self-congratulatory, high-dollar gathering that assures the DC establishment of its importance and strength. It also helps meld the press and the politician, the staffs of the powerful and the interview/comment machines that desperately need them. Those who weren't here likely aren't important. Those who were here know the rarified air they have breathed.[1]

Someone was missing, though. Only a few even noticed. They were not among the grandmothers and underwear models or the moms of receptionists or celebrity chefs. They did not arrive with the actresses, were certainly not with the personal assistants who clogged the halls. Nor did they accompany the woman a White House correspondent said was invited for "her breasts and her blogs, but mainly her breasts."

No. They were not here. Among the twenty-six hundred guests present this night, not one was a journalist who specializes in reporting religion. Not one. Not a single journalist at that dinner—a dinner specifically designed to celebrate all things news and Washington, DC—made it their life's work to inform the American people about the influence of faith in national affairs. There were people sipping chardonnay who are known for lengthy stories about the first lady's attire, but there was not a faith and culture, faith and politics, faith and anything writer to be found among the twenty-six hundred.

The White House Correspondents' Association could have invited Bob Smietana. He's the former president of the Religion Newswriters Association and a senior news editor for *Christianity Today*. He formerly wrote for the *Nashville Tennessean*, the paper where John Seigenthaler, David Halberstam, and Al Gore honed their craft.

Cathleen Falsani should have been sent an invitation. She looks good in a dress. She has worked for the *Chicago Tribune* and for *Religion Dispatches* at the University of Southern California. Her 2004 interview with Barack Obama is one of the most important in the history of presidential faith.

Paul Raushenbush probably owns a tux. He's the former associate dean of religious life at Princeton University and the executive editor of global spirituality and religion for *Huffington Post*. Arianna Huffington could have asked someone for a favor and gotten him in.

Lauren Green of *FOX News* would have done the event justice. She's both a faith journalist and a former runner-up Miss America. Jaweed Kaleem at *CNN* is an award-winning writer, as well as a Henry Luce Fellow in global religion at the International Center for Journalists. There are dozens of others: Sarah Pulliam Bailey of the *Washington Post* and Tom Gjelten of *National Public Radio* and Rachel Zoll of the *Associated Press*, to name a few.

Yet no room was found for them—not even one seat among three thousand.

It is, disturbingly, a common occurrence. It does not happen only at star-spangled dinners. There is also no room for religion reporters on the buses of presidential candidates. In fact, rarely are religion reporters even assigned to national campaigns. A very few will gain access to major events, but this is far more likely to happen if the pope or the Dalai Lama is in town. There is rarely time in a president's or a candidate's schedule for those who write about religion. Candidates routinely pass them on to their heads of "faith outreach." Even their own newspapers are often unsure of how to assign religion reporters. This is largely because advertisers and readers rarely get excited about the religion section of the paper. Isn't that where they announce church bazaars?

The neglect showed, tragically, nowhere more than during the 2012 presidential campaign. In that race, a Mormon Republican presidential candidate, the first of his faith to be a party nominee, ran against a sitting president whose faith story had played a decisive role in his initial presidential race in 2008. During that race, Mr. Obama had never stopped talking about how his faith inspired his policies. Surely then, in 2012, faith themes would be front and center. Surely they would be much aired and much debated. Surely this is what the times demanded, the faiths involved required, and the candidates themselves expected. Of course 2012 would be a high-water mark for religion reporting in America.

Yet it wasn't.

The statistics tell the pitiful story. The Pew Research Center concluded that only 6 percent of stories about that election made any reference to religion. Nearly 5 percent of that coverage was about a single event: the time a Baptist minister in Texas called Mitt Romney's Mormon religion a cult, which happened a full year before the election![2]

There was a reason for this meager attention to religion in 2012. Neither presidential candidate wanted to talk about it. Only one in seven religion-related stories in that heated race began with either of the campaigns. Religion reporters were left to themselves to think up angles that readers might like. That's the reason 30 percent of the reporting on religion during the 2012 campaign was about how white evangelicals would vote.[3] This is not the kind of thing candidates want to talk about or readers ask to hear more about. This is the kind of stuff journalists write about when trying to get some traction.

Religion simply didn't receive the serious attention the 2012 election required. Even the voters said so. After it was all over, 82 percent of Americans said they had learned "not very much" or "nothing at all" about the Mormon religion. More than a quarter of the US population still thought Obama was a Muslim. Almost no one learned anything about how religion might impact the presidency. This was because only 16 percent of all religion coverage dealt with the vital issue of how religion would impact policies or governing.[4]

In the years after that election, faith coverage continued to decline. Faith as a factor in politics continued to rise. Religion reporters were in trouble. The headlines told the tale. When religion writer Michael Paulson left the religion beat of the *New York Times* for the theater beat, one news outlet's headline was "Another One Bites the Dust? New York Times Religion Writer Taking His Talents to Broadway."[5] When more journalists specializing in faith found other work, the *American Conservative* asked, "Why Are Newspaper Religion Reporters Quitting?"[6] It got so bad that when the industry-leading Poynter Institute announced in a headline, "Three Religion Reporters Leave Dailies," it was compelled to add, "but the Job Isn't Vanishing."[7] Few in the trade were assured.

This trend continued well into the start of the 2016 presidential race. Again, religion played a role. One candidate announced his run at the chapel service of one of the most fundamentalist Christian colleges in the country. Nearly all candidates claimed that religion determined their approach to policy issues, abortion in particular—a matter moved to center stage by the release of video recordings purporting to expose organ-harvesting practices by Planned Parenthood. One candidate claimed that religion is at the heart of a woman's decision to seek an abortion. Every candidate and the sitting president claimed religion shaped their view of same-sex marriage. Indeed, every contender for the White House at the start of the 2016 race claimed profound religious underpinnings.

The state of the union of religion and politics in America is clear. Religion is thriving. The nation's politics are as faith-based as ever. Yet reporting on religion is near an all-time low—and there is much the voters still need to know.

It does seem that at least one seat could have been found for a religion reporter at the most important press and politics event in the nation's capital. Just one?

# Introduction

I go the way that Providence dictates with the assurance
of a sleepwalker.

Adolf Hitler

His name was Auguste. His parents preferred Isidore. He once signed
a legal document as "Brutus Napoleon."

He was an odd man. In 1824, he began a common-law marriage
to a woman about to be arrested for prostitution. The union lasted
eighteen years and was an agonizing disaster. He later proclaimed
it "the only error of my life." Humility was not among his gifts.

He was a cantankerous soul, often at the edge of sanity. After a
rebellious childhood, he became secretary and "spiritually adopted
son" to a famous philosopher. The two fought and eventually parted
company over which of them should receive credit for their work.
Episodes like this deepened the depression that deformed his life.
He was repeatedly hospitalized for mental illness and once tried to
kill himself by jumping from a bridge.

He made what living he could as a lecturer and writer. Poverty and
hardship filled his days. The woman he regarded as his muse died
horribly the same year he met her. His grief left him imbalanced. He

27

decided upon a course of "cerebral hygiene" during which he refused to allow the inferior thoughts of others to enter his mind. In time, he declared himself the high priest of his own religion.

He might have left this life unmourned and unremembered, just another unremarkable madman slipping quietly into eternity. Yet by the time he died in 1857, some of his ideas had begun to change the world.

★  ★  ★

He was certain, for example, that the scientific study of society would solve the problems of mankind. No more the tyranny of religion, philosophy, and tradition. Men of science must rule, he believed. Their exacting methods would solve the problems of the world and lead humanity into a golden age. This certainty became known as positivism. It was fruit of the turbulent mind of our beleaguered visionary Auguste Comte, the father of sociology.[1]

Among all that he will be remembered for—and there is much—one prediction in particular has profoundly shaped the modern world. Comte was thoroughly convinced that mankind would eventually evolve beyond religion. Indeed, he believed that a world free of religion was dawning even in his day.

He taught that human history began in a theological stage, an era marked by faith in gods and supernatural happenings. Despising religion as he did, Comte called this the fictitious stage. Then came a metaphysical stage in which philosophy ruled the minds of men. Ultimately, he believed, humanity would step into the positive or scientific stage. Men would discard their infantile fascination with religion and other misguided ideas. They would devote themselves instead to logical solutions for all the wrongs that beset the human race. Religion would dissolve forever in the brilliant light of a new and scientific age.

It was an idea that set minds aflame. A world without religion! A world ruled only by scientific fact! A world untroubled by prophets and priests, free of gods and supernatural concerns!

It was a vision that enflamed the mind of Karl Marx, among many others, shaping his vision of a world remade by revolution. It also put fire into the mind of John Stuart Mill and through him into the heart of the Victorian age. It found its way into such diverse places as the novels of Thomas Hardy and George Eliot and the thinking of Kemal Atatürk, the father of modern Turkey.

★  ★  ★

This confidence in the death of religion fashioned the way millions came to view the future, particularly in universities and among the ruling classes. The modern would be secular. The modern would be scientific. Comte had predicted it all.

And we believed. We had to. Our sociology professors told us it was true.

Yet Comte's prediction is among the greatest miscalculations in the history of ideas. It has left Western society largely uninformed, inept, and ineffective in dealing with one of the most defining forces in the modern world: religion.

The truth is that religion has not faded from history, nor is it in danger of doing so. There is no indication that mankind will one day abandon faith forever. In fact, the trends of our times indicate quite the opposite. The Islamic world is exploding in nearly every way. The Russian Orthodox Church is undergoing an unexpected resurrection.[2] Pentecostalism is dramatically on the rise in South America. Druidism, Wicca, and neo-pagan religions are sweeping through Europe. Christianity is expanding exponentially in China and sub-Saharan Africa. In some regions of the world, Roman Catholicism has survived its recent scandals and is thriving. Even ancient and otherworldly Hinduism and Buddhism are holding their own.

Were Comte alive he would be stunned—and widely criticized for getting it so wrong.

Nowhere is this more so than in the United States, where Comte's intellectual heirs have long predicted the demise of faith. As early as 1880, leading atheist Robert Ingersoll declared, "The churches are dying out all over the land."[3] These words were badly timed. Within decades, two religious movements arose from American soil and spread throughout the world: Pentecostalism and fundamentalism. American churches didn't die out. They multiplied.

Still came the dire predictions. In the middle of the next century, a new generation of experts announced, "God is dead." These words were intended as the secular benediction for a departed age of faith. Esteemed sociologist Peter Berger wrote that by "the twenty-first century, religious believers are likely to be found only in small sects, huddled together to resist a worldwide secular culture."[4] Anthropologist Anthony Wallace went further, assuring that the "evolutionary future of religion is extinction. . . . Belief in supernatural powers is doomed to die out, all over the world."[5] These warnings—perhaps they were hopes—and others like them have echoed endlessly ever since, particularly in American university classrooms.

Yet none of it has proven true. The United States is today among the most religious nations in the world. Some experts doubt this simply because American religion is changing forms. It is morphing along generational lines, remaking itself in the image of the young as it does. Yet whatever the trends—whatever recent shifts in church attendance, immigration, sexual ethics, and cultural influence have occurred—it is an undeniable fact that the vast majority of Americans are, in some form, religious.[6]

There are some Americans today, then, who are best described as the stunned descendants of Comte. They live in shock that religion still plays any role in American society, American politics in particular. Disappointment descends upon them each time a faith rears its unfashionable head. They view the religiously devoted as holdovers from a bygone era, anachronisms who keep all things American from evolving into their destined, religion-free state.

Nothing scares Comte's heirs like these religious Americans. They are a tribe apart, citizens of another world, worshipers who cling not only to God but also to far different predictions about religion and the nation's future than those proclaimed by Comte. They are foreign and at the same time deeply embedded in the flow of American history. When G. K. Chesterton wrote a century ago of "a nation with the soul of a church," he was thinking of Americans like these.[7]

This tribe is not disappointed by the presence of religion in modern American life. Instead, they celebrate it as the intended way, the fulfillment of the founding vision. They cannot forget that the Pilgrims sailed to the New World "for the glory of God and the advancement of the Christian faith."[8] They are comforted that it was on an "altar of God" that Thomas Jefferson swore "eternal hostility against every form of tyranny over the mind of man."[9] They understand why Lincoln was driven to his knees "by the overwhelming conviction I had nowhere else to go" and why Barack Obama would echo Lincoln a century and a half later.[10]

These Americans delight in every piece of evidence for an historic national faith. They take pride in the fact that signers of the Declaration of Independence relied "on the protection of divine Providence" as they affirmed rights endowed by a Creator. It seems completely natural to them that the First Congress approved an ordinance extolling "religion and morality" as "necessary to good government and the happiness of mankind."[11] Nor are they surprised that many of the monuments in their nation's capital, the motto inscribed on their money, and even the oath they take in court all assume the existence of God. This is merely what comes of having a church at the soul of the nation, in Chesterton's reworked phrase.

When religion surfaces in American politics, this tribe is grateful. They would wish nothing else, be disturbed by anything less. It is why they cannot envision electing an atheist to the presidency and are willing to entrust themselves politically only to men and women who believe in God. This is as it has always been, they believe. It is in keeping with the way of the fathers, with the founding faith of the land.

We Americans find ourselves, then, a feuding family born of very different parents. We were sired by visions of both the sacred and the secular. We descend from both the Renaissance and the Reformation. We are children of both Comte the atheist prophet and George Washington the Christian warrior. We are the siblings of both the outspoken skeptic Bill Maher and the outspoken evangelical Rick Warren. We find ourselves the parents of both students who wish to pray at football games and, well, Miley Cyrus.

This all leads us to a great mystery. It is a mystery that reveals itself constantly in American politics, every four years during presidential campaigns in particular. That mystery is this: Why are Americans so unwilling to demand religious clarity from their presidential candidates?

It is a mystery that seems—somehow—un-American. We would expect that those who harbor Comtean, secular hopes in their hearts would scour every religious pronouncement by a presidential candidate in order to fiercely demand exactitude and explanation. We would expect religious Americans to demand this same exactitude and explanation, though in their case for the sake of assuring orthodoxy and then taking up the cause. In other words, we would expect the secular to take religious statements by candidates seriously because they think them untrue. We would also expect religious Americans to take such statements seriously because they think they might be true. Either way, religious statements by presidential candidates ought to be among the most scrutinized and debated of all political pronouncements.

They aren't. Instead, presidential campaigns are filled with pious mush, airy declarations of faith, and broad-brush assurances of devotion that go largely unscrutinized. We hardly hear them anymore. All candidates assure the voters of their faith. Every candidate offers the required phrases: "God bless America" at the end of a speech or "With God's help we will march forward." Few candidates offer—and fewer still are asked to offer—any reasonable explanation of what they believe. We are left with feelings more than facts, intimations more than concrete beliefs.

Yet behind the usual religious gush of the campaign are core beliefs and years of defining experience. The gush conceals the reality—and sometimes the genuine soul—of the candidate. We do not want our politicians to act like theologians to appease us. We do not want to invade their prayers. We do, though, want to understand the inner compass of those we elect to power. The truth is that we seldom do.

The great oddity of this is that we live in a shockingly intrusive media culture. Nearly every detail of a political candidate's life is now put fully on display. It is nothing today for the entire nation to know what kind of underwear a presidential candidate prefers. We may also be required to know, whether we wish to or not, the name of a candidate's dog, the song that was playing at the dawn of first love, the outcome of recent medical exams, and even the circumstances of lost virginity. Yet most Americans would not dare expect this same degree of detail about a presidential candidate's religious beliefs—beliefs that could lead the nation into war, upend economies, or transform culture.

It is all difficult to explain. Some say the fault is in our manners. We Americans tend to think religion is a private matter and that no one should be pressed publicly about what they believe. Perhaps this makes us unwilling to grill political candidates about their faith.

Others say this tendency in our culture comes from our understanding of the First Amendment. If church and state are to be separate, then perhaps personal faith and governing should be too. Maybe it doesn't matter what a candidate believes. He isn't supposed to take his faith with him into office anyway.

A more cynical view is that we don't take political candidates seriously when they talk about religion, and so we've long ceased to care what they say. Or it could be that the silence of voters about religion in presidential campaigns is a result of our national ignorance about religion as a whole. Surveys often show that Americans barely know what their own faith teaches, much less the relevant details of religions not their own.[12]

Whatever the cause, we cannot afford to leave faith unexamined among those aspiring to the highest office in our land. Religion not only has proven too influential upon what most presidents do in office but also plays too great a role in the crises of our age to be ignored.

In recent decades, Americans have watched as a president reversed his position on same-sex marriage and cited the Sermon on the Mount as a reason. Another president appealed to a distinctly Christian definition of "just war" prior to deploying US forces in Muslim lands. A president has cited the Koran in urging legislation pertaining to the poor, the Bhagavad Gita in contending for immigration policy, and the Torah in arguing for economic reform. One president questioned whether atheists are qualified to hold US citizenship. Religious principle has directly shaped what presidents have done about prison reform, about abortion, about welfare, about capital punishment, and about a host of other vital national issues.

Perhaps this is as it should be. Perhaps it is not. Yet none of it ought to occur without voter scrutiny, without prior knowledge, without the open forums, media examination, and insistence upon clarity that befit American democracy in an age of religious fervor. Without these, religion can come close to being an unelected co-president. It can become an unknown and unanticipated factor in the decision-making of the most powerful official in the world.

★　★　★

This urgent need for understanding the faith of presidential candidates is all the more pressing given our postmodern culture. We are a generation that does not accept unaltered the faiths delivered from our ancestors. Instead, we customize, we refashion, we make religion our own. We give old faiths new purpose, old words new meaning—or a variety of meanings.

This can make labels obsolete, or at least unhelpful. What does it mean for a candidate to declare himself a Roman Catholic, for example? Will he oppose abortion rights, or same-sex marriage, or legalized marijuana, or distributing condoms in public schools? Will the pope be of influence in his decision-making? Will Catholicism be merely the most influential of several religions that color the lens through which this candidate views the world? What if the candidate is a Methodist? Can we know anything about his views from this word alone? Or the word *evangelical*? What does it tell us? There was a time when the labels largely told the tale. Now they fail us. We have to "ask the question."

This will be no easier in the years to come. As these words are being written, there are a Muslim and a Hindu in the US Congress. There are also several "nones." We can expect people of each of these faiths to one day run for president. Yet what is the Muslim approach to gay marriage? Is there a Hindu approach to governing? Or are there many Hindu approaches to governing? Can we know from the name alone anything about how a "none" will lead?

Again, we will have to "ask the question." We will have to demand clarity. We will have to insist that we understand the influence of religion on the lives of presidential candidates before they take office.

★　★　★

Comte was wrong. He left us unprepared for the age in which we live. We can forgive him.[13] Generations of his academic disciples were equally wrong. It is understandable. What will be neither forgivable nor understandable is if our generation of Americans, with all the evidence amassed before us, continues to allow religion in American politics to be the sentimental, barely comprehensible, shadowy thing it has been. Those in Munich who heard Adolf Hitler speak the words that began this chapter eventually wished they had asked more questions. We, too, must ask the questions of faith that need to be asked. It is time for the mysteries, the uncertainties, and the gambling with the nation's future to end.

★　★　★

## A Personal Word

I first entered the contentious arena of American faith and politics in 2003 when I wrote *The Faith of George W. Bush*. It was a book designed to fill a void. Americans knew that Mr. Bush's presidency was among the most faith-based in their history, but they did not know the contours of that faith. The president, who was just then seeking a second term, had absorbed his family's insistence that religion is a private matter. He said little about his faith, and what he did say was famously unclear. His administration's spokespersons were thus forced into silence about matters of faith, and this left both his supporters and his critics sometimes frustrated and often unsure.

36

My book helped to ease this frustration, and I was grateful. Yet I believed then as I believe now that its most important contribution was not the recounting of Bush's religious journey but its insistence that faith can define a presidency by first defining the soul of the one who becomes president. As I wrote in the introduction to *The Faith of George W. Bush*, "An underlying assumption of this book is that a man's religion permeates all he does whether he knows it or not. What he believes works itself out practically in his life, so there is a connection between his view of grace and his garden, between his idea of Providence and his way of parenting."[14]

It was this view that led me to write *The Faith of Barack Obama* in 2008. Though Mr. Obama's faith was far different from the faith of George W. Bush, both men were, I believed, equally faith-based. To either stand with Obama or to defeat him, it was essential to understand the religious ideals that framed his life and politics.

His critics weren't having it. To them, Obama was at best a Muslim and at worst a man playing at Christianity to win votes. Their ire spilled over onto me. Speeches were canceled. My life was threatened. It was as though I had written a book extolling the virtues of the Antichrist.

Yet the book sold well, and the reason was that Americans were as mystified by Obama's faith as they had been by Bush's. The one was both guarded and inarticulate about his faith. The other was a confusing work in progress, a man who had been tutored by the theological radicalism of Jeremiah Wright for twenty years, had then parted company with his fiery pastor just before entering office, and soon after had welcomed theological conservatives and evangelicals among his closest spiritual advisors. Obama's faith was difficult to know, but Americans sensed it was an essential part of him. They were right.

Again, my book helped to clear the fog, but again, I was most interested in its underlying assumption. As I wrote in its pages, "If a man's faith is sincere, it is the most important thing about him, and it is impossible to understand who he is and how he will lead without first understanding the religious vision that informs his life."[15]

Among my more fascinating and enjoyable experiences in the wake of these two books were the many calls I received from journalists as they attempted to decode the meaning of religion in American politics. If someone spoke of George W. Bush as being "anointed," a friend at the *New York Times* would inevitably call and say something like, "Look, I'm Jewish. It sounds to me like the man is anointing himself king. What's going on?" A journalist in the Middle East read Barack Obama's "Call to Renewal" speech and came upon the conversion story in which Obama says, "I didn't fall out." Then came the call: "What eez theez 'fell out'? Stephen, I ask you. Is theez what I see weeth Benny Hinn on American TV?" These conversations and dozens like them are among my most cherished memories of those days.

Since that time I coauthored a book about the faith of Sarah Palin and wrote another about Mormonism during Mitt Romney's presidential campaign. For perspective, I also wrote about Abraham Lincoln's religious struggles and their impact on his presidency and the country.

What has emerged from my years as a student of religion in American politics—from a thousand interviews, hundreds of articles, and dozens of debates—are three certainties. First, there is beauty to a life informed by faith that is inspiring to behold. This alone rewards the investment in time and study. Second, there is an ignorance of religion in our generation that has become a threat of its own. Confusion and uncertainty about religion envelop voters, journalists, and aspiring statesmen alike. We can fix this. Whatever the cause of this confusion and uncertainty—Comte, laziness, a misreading of the First Amendment—our institutions and our educators are capable of offering a remedy. May it happen soon. The need is urgent given the faith factor in the crises of our time.

Finally, I am more convinced now than when I first began that there is an inherent connection between faith and public policy, between belief and governing. In order to make laws and policies, we first ask ourselves about what is right, what is fair, and what is true. Action springs from the answer to the question, "What ought to be done?" These are often religious questions, matters of faith and values rather than of science and laboratory certainties. It means that faiths of various kinds will always shape governing, so we must know the nature of those faiths before the governing begins. It is the obligation that falls to a democratic people who are heirs to the kind of legacy of freedom our national parents left us.

Ours is not a secular age. It is an age of faith. We should conduct ourselves so as to navigate its currents skillfully.

Though I am grateful to have made my contributions in this field, there is much more to be done. Better minds and writers than I must enlist in this cause. Many have, and we should be thankful. The role of religion in American politics should be the subject of careful analysis and reasoned debate, not just the stuff of cable news screamfests as it often is today. Religion is not going away. It is shaping our world. We may not like it. We may not understand it. Yet it rules us all the same. Better that we awaken from our dreams of a secular world to contend with the world as it truly is.

# PROFILE

## FORTY-NINE TRUTHS ABOUT RELIGION IN AMERICA

1. There are slightly more than 320 million people currently living in the United States.
2. Approximately 92% of Americans believe in God.[1]
3. 70.6% of all Americans are Christians of some kind.[2]
4. 25.4% of all Americans are evangelical Christians.
5. 20.8% of all Americans are Roman Catholic Christians.
6. 14.7% of all Americans are mainline Protestant Christians.
7. 6.5% of all Americans are historically black Protestant Christians.
8. 0.5% of all Americans are Eastern Orthodox Christians of some kind.
9. 22.8% of all Americans are unaffiliated or religious "nones."
10. 3.1% of all Americans are atheists.
11. 4.0% of all Americans are agnostics.
12. 15.8% of all Americans report that they are "nothing in particular" with regard to religion.

13. 1.9% of all Americans are Jewish.

14. 0.9% of all Americans are Muslim.

15. 0.7% of all Americans are Buddhist.

16. 0.7% of all Americans are Hindu.

17. 0.6% of all Americans report that in religious matters the best description of them is "don't know."

18. Racial and ethnic minorities comprise 41% of all Catholics, 24% of all evangelicals, and 14% of all mainline Protestants.

19. Mormonism is the fastest-growing religion in America.

20. Evangelicals are the fastest-growing Christian religion in America.

21. Jews are the wealthiest religious group in America; 44% of their households earn more than $100,000 a year.

22. Hindus are the best-educated religious group in America. Nearly half hold graduate degrees. Fully 77% are college graduates.

23. The marriage rate by US religious groups is highest among Mormons (66%); others of note include Jewish (56%), mainline and evangelical Protestant (55% each), Catholic (52%), Muslim (41%), and historically black Protestant (31%).[3]

24. Approximately 83% of older Americans are Christian; half of Americans eighteen to thirty years of age are Christian, and a third identify as "nones."

25. Muslims are the youngest and most male religious group in America.

26. The median age of all Muslims is twenty-eight.[4]

27. 44% of adult Muslims in the United States are between the ages of eighteen and twenty-nine, compared with 17% for evangelical Protestants and Catholics.[5]

28. 65% of the US Muslim population is male and 35% is female, compared with a ratio in the general public of 48% male, 52%

female, and a ratio among evangelical Protestants of 45% male, 55% female.[6]

29. Hindus, Muslims, and Jews have the highest retention rate of members.

30. The median age of unaffiliated adults or "nones" in America is thirty-six.

31. The median age of mainline Protestants in America is fifty-two.

32. The median age of Roman Catholics in America is forty-nine.

33. One in seven Americans reads the Bible on a regular basis. Half of all Americans believe the Bible has too little influence on American culture.[7]

34. 49% of all Americans believe that churches and other houses of worship should express their views on social and political issues.

35. 46% of all Americans would not vote for an atheist for president.[8]

36. 18% of Americans would not vote for a Mormon presidential candidate.[9]

37. Fewer than half of all American adults can name the four Gospels of the New Testament.[10]

38. More than half of all American Christians believe some non-Christian religions can lead to eternal life.[11]

39. 54% of Republicans, 26% of independents, and 10% of Democrats believe that "deep down" Barack Obama is a Muslim.[12]

40. There are roughly 350,000 religious congregations in the US—314,000 are Protestant or other Christian, 24,000 are Catholic or Orthodox, and 12,000 are non-Christian.[13]

41. Average weekly US church attendance is 186.[14]

42. 50% of churchgoers attend the largest 10% of congregations in the United States.[15]

43. More than four thousand US churches close their doors each year.[16]

44. Each year 2.7 million church members fall into inactivity.[17]

45. The number of mosques in the US more than doubled from 1994 (962) to 2011 (2,106) and rose by 74% between 2000 and 2011.[18]

46. The average number of participants per mosque dropped from 1,625 in 2000 to 1,248 in 2011.[19]

47. By 2050, Muslims are projected to surpass religious Jews to become the second-largest US religion with 2.1% of the US population, up from 0.9% in 2010.

48. The percentage of the US population that is Christian is projected to decline by 2050 from 78.3% to 66.4%. Religiously unaffiliated Americans ("nones") are projected to rise from 22.8% to 25.6%. Religious Jews are projected to decline from 1.8% to 1.4%.[20]

49. By 2050, Hindus are projected to double as a share of the US population from 0.6% to 1.2%; Buddhists are expected to increase slightly from 1.2% to 1.4%.

# 1

# Kennedy at Houston

> Those who say religion has nothing to do with politics
> do not know what religion is.
>
> > Mahatma Gandhi

If there is a dividing line in the history of religion and American politics, it passes through September 12, 1960. It was on this date that Senator John F. Kennedy made a speech to the Greater Houston Ministerial Association in defense of the scandalous suggestion that a Roman Catholic could be president of the United States.

That speech has become the model for all similar religious declarations by political candidates in the years since. Whenever a candidate for president has felt the need to offer assurances about his faith, he has almost always invoked Kennedy at Houston, has usually given the speech in Texas, and has nearly always made sure there were large numbers of Southern clergy in the room at the time. This is what Mitt Romney did when his Mormonism became an issue in the 2008 presidential campaign, and it is what we will see future candidates

45

do when their particular brands of religion raise questions in the minds of American voters.

Though Kennedy's Houston speech served the purposes of his campaign, it is a model that does not serve us well today. His words were aimed at a far different target in a centuries-old religious war far removed from the religious battle lines in current American politics. Understanding this will help us determine what the greater need is in our day and why it is essential that we ask our presidential candidates penetrating questions of faith.

The roiling animosities that threatened John F. Kennedy's presidential campaign first arose between Protestants and Roman Catholics during the Reformation and crashed onto the shores of the New World with the earliest American colonies. Many of the first settlers in these colonies were refugees from the rule of England's last Roman Catholic king, James II, or from the persecutions of Protestants in France that followed the revocation of the Edict of Nantes. These colonists read their King James Bibles, their *Foxe's Book of Martyrs*, and even their Shakespeare and were confirmed in their confidence that Roman Catholicism was an enemy of biblical truth, of liberty, and even of art and the creative aspirations of the human soul.

By the time the American founding fathers signed the Declaration of Independence, only thirty thousand Catholics lived in the new nation—less than 1 percent of the total population. Most of them lived in Maryland, a colony established for the protection of persecuted British Catholics. There were no Catholic churches south of Maryland.

Catholics were so suspect that some prominent founders wondered if they should be citizens. John Jay, who was both the first chief justice of the United States and an author of *The Federalist Papers*, argued that the Constitution of New York ought to exclude

Catholics from citizenship unless they repented of their belief in transubstantiation and their allegiance to the pope.[1] This was despite the fact that two Roman Catholics, Charles Carroll of Maryland and Daniel Fitzsimmons of Pennsylvania, were signers of the Declaration of Independence.

A tense peace reigned in Protestant/Catholic relations until the 1830s, when Catholic immigrants, many of them Irish, began arriving in huge numbers. Heated competition for wealth and influence divided old settlers from new. Ancient animosities erupted, and violence ensued. Riots spilled into the streets of American cities and tore through Catholic neighborhoods. Catholic churches were burned. Catholic students were beaten in public schools for refusing to use the Protestant version of the Bible and the Protestant rendering of the Lord's Prayer.[2]

Hating Catholics became politically popular. The Know Nothing Party prevailed in more than one state largely because of its resistance to "the followers of Rome." President Ulysses S. Grant even predicted that the new divide in the United States would be not between slave and free sentiments but between Protestant and Catholic—a tension he described as "between patriotism and intelligence on the one side, and superstition, ambition, and ignorance on the other."[3]

As late as 1884, a presidential campaign turned on a charge of "rum, Romanism, and rebellion."[4] Even the usually measured Theodore Roosevelt declared that the Catholic Church "is in no way suited to this country and can never have any great permanent growth except through immigration, for its thought is Latin and entirely at variance with the dominant thought of our country and institutions."[5] In 1916, philosopher George Santayana took the point further in an article for the *New Republic*: "If . . . the Catholic church ever became dominant in America, it would without doubt . . . transform American life and institutions. . . . It would abolish religious liberty, the freedom of the press, divorce, and lay education."[6]

★   ★   ★

Clearly, the brand of religious bigotry John F. Kennedy faced in the 1960s was not new. It had already landed upon Al Smith, the first Roman Catholic candidate for president, in the 1920s. Of Smith's battles Eleanor Roosevelt later wrote, "The kind of propaganda that some of the religious groups, aided and abetted by the opposition, put forth in that campaign utterly disgusted me. If I need anything to show me what prejudice can do to the intelligence of human beings, that campaign was the best lesson I could have had."[7]

Perhaps a more soft-spoken, less overt Roman Catholic candidate could have quieted the storm. This wasn't Al Smith. He was blunt, bludgeoning, and unapologetic, particularly about his faith. During his New York political career, he made numerous well-publicized trips to the Vatican, where Pope Pius XI gave him glowing praise. It did not endear Smith to Protestants back home. As governor of New York, Smith prominently displayed a painting of the pope and once even publically kissed a cardinal's ring. A popular Methodist bishop was incensed: "No governor can kiss the papal ring and get within gun shot of the White House."[8]

And so it began. In 1927, a Protestant lawyer wrote an open letter to Smith that appeared in *Atlantic Monthly*. The lawyer demanded to know whether Smith's devotion to the Roman Catholic Church did not amount to a dual loyalty that would force him to decide between American democracy and various papal encyclicals on church-state relations.

Upon reading the article, Smith turned to his aides and shouted, "What the hell is a papal encyclical?" In time, he agreed to answer the charges in *Atlantic Monthly*. It did little good. Though it is unlikely that even a Protestant Smith could have defeated the popular Herbert Hoover, anti-Catholic sentiment swept the country and crushed Smith politically and personally.

The bias against him was well summarized by Mrs. Willie W. Caldwell, a leading Republican Party voice from Virginia. As she wrote to the women of her state, "Mr. Hoover himself and the National Committee are depending on the women to save our country in this hour of vital moral religious crisis. We must save the United States from being Romanized, and rum-ridden, and the call is to the women to do something."[9]

This kind of inflamed rhetoric helped turn the 1928 election into a rout. Herbert Hoover won 58 percent of the popular vote and 444 of the 521 Electoral College votes. Rumors swirled that when Al Smith learned of his trouncing, he wrote a one-word telegram to the Vatican. It said simply, "Unpack."

★   ★   ★

Passions of the kind arrayed against Al Smith in the 1920s had abated little by the time John F. Kennedy decided to run for president in 1959. Both Kennedy and the millions of Americans who supported him hoped it might be otherwise. The young senator had won reelection by a huge margin. He was an outspoken champion of progressive causes. Unlike Smith, he was handsome, suave, and articulate. He was educated in secular schools, including Harvard University. He had also been awarded the Pulitzer Prize for his book *Profiles in Courage*. Kennedy and those who admired him thought his gifts and his achievements would keep his religion from being used as a weapon against him.

It didn't prove true. Kennedy met fierce religious opposition from the moment he announced his candidacy. In November 1959, the Texas Baptist Commission "adopted a resolution cautioning members . . . against voting for a Roman Catholic candidate." Alabama Baptists did the same soon after. So did the National Association of Evangelicals. W. A. Criswell, pastor of the influential First Baptist Church of Dallas, seemed the champion for a growing number of

American Protestants. In a much-quoted sermon, Criswell spoke of "Roman Catholicism's bloody hand" and warned that Kennedy's election would "spell the death of a free church in a free state and our hopes of continuance of full religious liberty in America."[10]

Constantly at issue was the charge that the Roman Catholic Church was not merely a religious organization but a foreign state. The influential magazine *Christianity Today* insisted that "Protestant voters not at all irrationally would prefer to keep the White House out of the hands of someone who confesses to a foreign earthly power." Alabama Methodists agreed, declaring, "The people of Alabama do not intend to jeopardize their liberties by opening the doors of the White House to the political machinations of a determined power-hungry Romanist hierarchy."[11]

These concerns reached their crescendo in the fall of 1960 when 150 religious leaders met at Washington's Mayflower Hotel. Though largely religious conservatives, their spokesman was Norman Vincent Peale, author of *The Power of Positive Thinking* and minister at a Fifth Avenue church in Manhattan. After a one-day conference, the group issued a statement declaring it "inconceivable that a Roman Catholic president would not be under extreme pressure by the hierarchy of his church to accede to its policies."[12]

Expressing the sense of urgency about opposing Kennedy that pervaded the conference, Peale later said, "Our American culture is at stake. . . . I don't say it won't survive, but it won't be what it was."[13] Statements like these moved Adlai Stevenson to revive an old quip: "In this campaign it seems as if each party has a patron saint. Personally, I must admit that I find St. Paul appealing and St. Peale appalling."[14]

Opposition to Kennedy's Catholicism did not come only from religious conservatives. The leading anti-Catholic voice of the time was Paul Blanshard, the legal counsel for an organization called Protestants and Other Americans United for the Separation of Church and State. He had written a book entitled *American Freedom and Catholic Power*, which called for a "resistance movement" to the Catholic Church in order to answer its "antidemocratic social policies of the hierarchy."[15] Blanshard targeted Catholic schools as "the most important divisive instrument in the life of American children" and claimed these schools produced the majority of "white criminals."[16] Surprisingly, the book was a bestseller and a Book of the Month Club selection. It was endorsed by John Dewey, Bertrand Russell, McGeorge Bundy, and Albert Einstein.[17]

The mounting concern over Kennedy's Catholicism seemed to confirm a Gallup poll conducted early in the campaign. It reported that when voters became aware of Kennedy's faith, he lost 7 percent of his support.[18] This was a large enough margin to make all the difference in swing states like West Virginia, Michigan, Missouri, and Texas.

Kennedy's opportunity to address the religious controversy swirling about his campaign arrived with an invitation from the Greater Houston Ministerial Association. Would he speak to them and clarify his views? Kennedy and his staff knew it could be a defining moment. The address would be timely—September 12, 1960, just as the general election moved to the center of the national stage. There would be a thousand ministers in attendance, most of them from among the Southern Baptists who opposed him so fiercely. It would be televised. It would be in Texas. Kennedy needed Texas.

★   ★   ★

As with nearly all of Kennedy's major addresses, many hands worked and reworked the language of the Houston speech. The gifts of senior speechwriter Ted Sorensen are particularly evident. Yet it was Kennedy's own sense of the moment that swayed minds and won hearts that historic Monday evening at the Rice Hotel in Houston. As John Seigenthaler later recalled, "Kennedy knew he was in enemy territory both politically and religiously. He knew the entire campaign could turn in a few minutes. I never saw him as brilliant as he was then."[19]

That night the candidate was introduced. After a few opening comments and some light campaigning, he warmed to his topic.

I believe in an America where the separation of church and state is absolute, where no Catholic prelate would tell the president (should he be Catholic) how to act, and no Protestant minister would tell his parishioners for whom to vote; where no church or church school is granted any public funds or political preference; and where no man is denied public office merely because his religion differs from the president who might appoint him or the people who might elect him.

I believe in an America that is officially neither Catholic, Protestant, nor Jewish; where no public official either requests or accepts instructions on public policy from the pope, the National Council of Churches, or any other ecclesiastical source; where no religious body seeks to impose its will directly or indirectly upon the general populace or the public acts of its officials; and where religious liberty is so indivisible that an act against one church is treated as an act against all. . . .

That is the kind of America in which I believe. And it represents the kind of presidency in which I believe—a great office that must neither be humbled by making it the instrument of any one religious group nor tarnished by arbitrarily withholding its occupancy from the members of any one religious group. I believe in a president whose religious views are his own private affair, neither imposed by him upon the nation or imposed by the nation upon him as a condition to holding that office.

Kennedy's language became more personal as he entered the latter half of the speech. He offered the assurances he knew his audience hoped to hear.

But let me stress again that these are my views. For contrary to common newspaper usage, I am not the Catholic candidate for president. I am the Democratic Party's candidate for president who happens also to be a Catholic. I do not speak for my church on public matters, and the church does not speak for me.

Whatever issue may come before me as president—on birth control, divorce, censorship, gambling, or any other subject—I will make my decision in accordance with these views, in accordance with what my conscience tells me to be the national interest, and without regard to outside religious pressures or dictates. And no power or threat of punishment could cause me to decide otherwise.

The speech was vintage Kennedy. History attended on the wings of his words. Images of Virginia Anglicans persecuting Baptist dissenters during the colonial period formed in the room. More recent heroes like Konrad Adenauer of Germany and Charles de Gaulle, both Roman Catholics and both revered by Americans at the time, stepped to the fore. Having made sure to visit the Alamo earlier that day, Kennedy wrung tears from some in the audience by declaring, "Side by side with Bowie and Crockett died McCafferty and Bailey and Carey. But no one knows whether they were Catholic or not, for there was no religious test at the Alamo."

Ever the politician, he was careful to place himself within this heroic pageant. Using the very taunts of his critics, some of whom were sitting before him as he spoke, he said, "This is the kind of America I believe in, and this is the kind I fought for in the South Pacific, and the kind my brother died for in Europe. No one suggested then that we may have a 'divided loyalty,' that we did 'not believe in liberty,' or that we belonged to a disloyal group that threatened the 'freedoms for which our forefathers died.'"

As emotional as the speech was, Kennedy had not forgotten his purpose. At the end of the speech, after reminding all of the broader business at hand, he movingly recited the words he hoped to recite again before the entire country early the next year. They were the words of the presidential oath of office: "For without reservation, I can 'solemnly swear that I will faithfully execute the office of president of the United States, and will to the best of my ability preserve, protect, and defend the Constitution, so help me God.'"

The audience in Houston immediately rose in a standing ovation. The nation took note.

* * *

Whatever else may be said about Kennedy's speech in Houston, it did the job it was designed to do. In the national election two months later, Kennedy received 34 percent of the white Protestant vote. This was approximately the same percentage Adlai Stevenson, the previous Democratic candidate for president, had received. Yet Kennedy won 83 percent of the Catholic vote, far beyond Stevenson's 45 percent.[20] In his extremely tight race with Richard Nixon, Kennedy won because he both neutralized anti-Catholic fears and rallied Catholics—Republican Catholics in particular—to his cause. The Houston speech was decisive in this victory.

Still, it could not quell the religious furor of the campaign. Shortly after Houston, Robert Kennedy admitted, "Right now, religion is the biggest issue in the country."[21] As historian Patricia Barrett has written, "Many Americans thought that the worst extremes of bigotry and prejudice had been laid to rest alongside Al Smith's presidential aspirations in 1928. The record, however, shows that professional bigots were more active in 1960 than in 1928. The magnitude and virulence of the anti-Catholic material flooding the country reached unprecedented dimensions during the first week of November."[22]

Even elder statesmen entered the fray. Fiery ex-president Harry Truman fought hard for Kennedy and helped him win Missouri. Truman did this largely by confronting leaders of his own denomination. I "cussed out the Baptists," he reported proudly.

★ ★ ★

While most Catholics rejoiced in their newfound acceptance and rallied to the Democratic champion, their more thoughtful leaders realized what had happened. Kennedy had reassured the country about his faith by stepping away from it. Instead of allegiance to the Catholic Church, he had pledged allegiance to American "civil religion." This is a phrase scholars use to denote American ideals woven into a secular religion of the state. It is religious language ripped from its original context and applied to the American experience. Largely because of his Houston speech, some of these scholars have spoken of Kennedy as the high priest of American civil religion.

Catholic leaders were concerned. When Kennedy expressed in a 1959 *Look* magazine interview the same ideas he would offer in Houston a year later, the editors of the Jesuit magazine *American* were incredulous: "We were somewhat taken aback . . . by the unvarnished statement that 'whatever one's religion in his private life . . . nothing takes precedence over his oath. . . .' Mr. Kennedy doesn't really believe that. No religious man, be he Catholic, Protestant or Jew, holds such an opinion."[23]

Even Kennedy's closest friends in the clergy were disturbed. Archbishop Philip Hannan was such a valued advisor to the Kennedys that Mrs. Kennedy asked him to deliver the eulogy at her husband's funeral. Yet years later the ninety-seven-year-old archbishop recalled, "Though I was immensely privileged to have been his trusted friend and consultant, we didn't always agree on religious matters."[24] "From my perspective," the aging cleric recounted in his memoir, "Kennedy went overboard in emphasizing his independence from the Catholic Church, essentially promising an arms-length manifesto as well as a wall of separation between himself and the Church."[25]

What Catholic leaders concluded was what also concerned many Protestants. To appease concerns about the authority of the Roman

Catholic Church, Kennedy had appealed to the authority of the American experience, assuring voters that his faith would never taint his democratic beliefs. It was a verbal sleight of hand that worked for Kennedy in Houston, but its many reincarnations have merely served to obscure the truth about the influence of religion in the lives of presidential candidates.

Jacqueline Kennedy may have unknowingly rendered the final verdict about her husband and his faith. During the 1960 campaign, she was heard to say, "I think it's so unfair of people to be against Jack because he's Catholic. He's such a poor Catholic."[26]

As valuable as John Kennedy's Houston speech was to his campaign and as helpful as it was in easing anti-Catholic sentiment, it does not serve us well as a model today. This is not merely because Kennedy appealed to a form of American civic mysticism that has now lost its magic. It is because Kennedy was forced to address a charge that is rarely heard today. He had to answer for the influence of a religious institution—its reach, its subversive intentions, its supposedly tyrannical sway over American minds.

We should recall the language of those who feared a Kennedy presidency. The White House would be in the hands of "a foreign earthly power." A "power-hungry Romanist hierarchy" would rule the country. The "pope of Rome" would sit in "the presidential chair."

The concern was about the Roman Church as a political force, as a foreign state. How much was Kennedy its agent? How far did the tentacles of Rome intrude? What would the pope of Rome do once he ruled America?

These are not our concerns today. No one lost sleep over how far the Methodist Church might intrude into the presidency of George W. Bush. Many Americans expressed doubts about Barack Obama's religion, but the thought of a coup by the United Church of Christ held no terror. No one worried that a power-hungry Baptist hierarchy might rule the nation with Bill Clinton as its pawn. The Union was certainly safe from a Quaker uprising during the Nixon years.

Our concerns are—or ought to be—different. We are not threatened by religious institutions, religious orthodoxy, or religious conformity in the Oval Office. Quite the opposite. Our concern is—or ought to be—the informality of faith today. It is the patchwork of faith that a presidential candidate has fashioned for himself. It is what an aspiring president has taken from the faith buffet of our time, from the postmodern smorgasbord of religious options.

A US soldier in Iraq was asked in 2005 about his religion. He said, "Well, it's about two parts Sunday school, one part Deepak Chopra, a few parts Oprah, and a whole lot Nike and beer commercials."[27] This was more specific than most Americans will admit to, but the soldier's answer was very much in keeping with the religious trends of our time. We are a generation of religious entrepreneurs, spiritual creatives who distrust the rules and think nothing of supergluing disparate pieces of religion together in a manner that would never have occurred to earlier generations.

Some Americans arrive at this pastiche through study. Some arrive simply by blending together all the faiths that have offered them meaningful experience. Many acquire their beliefs in the same way they acquire colds—through casual contact with strangers. Whatever the method, Americans have become religious adventurers. The old definitions don't apply; the old boundaries don't define. We no longer join religions. We curate their parts into customized faiths of our own.

Perhaps we need not fear this. Perhaps we need not oppose. Yet once we come to the realm of politics, we must insist upon understanding the customized faiths of our presidential candidates before we place them into the most powerful position in the world.

This is why the example of Kennedy at Houston fails us. His crisis was one of institutional power. He answered it with the lessons of the American experience. His crisis is not our crisis, and his answers would not be deemed sufficient today. This is the reason that attempts to invoke Kennedy at Houston, to re-create the success of his speech in our day, usually fail miserably.

★   ★   ★

This was certainly the experience of Mitt Romney. As he stepped into the 2008 presidential race, Romney knew he had a "Mormon problem." Early polls showed that as much as 40 percent of the Republican base, many of them evangelicals, said they would not vote for a Mormon.[28] Other polls indicated that a huge number of Americans viewed Mormonism as a cult.

Romney's distaste for discussing his religion publicly had not served him well. Like Kennedy, he was an accomplished man who resented having to defend his faith as though it was some personal flaw, an embarrassing black mark on his otherwise sterling résumé.

Yet Romney had a problem Kennedy didn't: he had been as much a clergyman as it is possible to be in the Mormon Church. He had served as bishop of a ward, which meant he was the head of his congregation. He had also presided over the Boston Stake, which made him spiritual leader to more than four thousand fellow Mormons. He had given millions of dollars to fund Mormon facilities and programs.

Simply put, he was, whether he wished to be or not, one of the most prominent Mormons in the world. Resent it as he might, Romney would have to face his Mormon problem head-on if he had any chance of reaching the Oval Office. The need of the moment was an explanation of what Romney believed. What did it mean to be a Mormon? What would it mean for the nation if a Mormon sat in the Oval Office? Most Americans simply didn't know enough about Romney's religion to even guess at an answer.

58

They had seen the bicycle-riding Mormon missionaries with white shirts and impeccable manners in their neighborhoods. They probably knew the names of some prominent Mormons—management gurus like Steven Covey, hotel magnates like J. Willard Marriott, airline presidents like David Needleman of JetBlue, and CEOs of global corporations like Gary Crittenden of American Express and Michael Bertasso of Heinz. They certainly knew of the Osmond family and of media personalities like Glenn Beck.

None of it helped America understand Mormonism. In fact, polls showed that most Americans who were likely to vote knew little about the Latter-Day Saints and what they did know made them suspect the religion.[29] Romney would have to bridge this divide.

He decided to answer his critics and the concerned on December 6, 2007, in a speech at the George Bush Presidential Library in College Station, Texas. After a kind introduction by former president George H. W. Bush, Romney began his "Faith in America" speech.

Understanding both his task and his moment in history, Romney quickly invoked the memory of Kennedy at Houston.

> Almost fifty years ago another candidate from Massachusetts explained that he was an American running for president, not a Catholic running for president. Like him, I am an American running for president. I do not define my candidacy by my religion. A person should not be elected because of his faith, nor should he be rejected because of his faith.

Also like Kennedy, Romney gave the guarantees he knew his audience required.

> Let me assure you that no authorities of my church, or of any other church for that matter, will ever exert influence on presidential decisions. Their authority is theirs, within the province of church affairs, and it ends where the affairs of the nation begin.

As governor, I tried to do the right as best I knew it, serving the law and answering to the Constitution. I did not confuse the particular teachings of my church with the obligations of the office and of the Constitution—and of course, I would not do so as president. I will put no doctrine of any church above the plain duties of the office and the sovereign authority of the law.

Then, as it had been in 1960, history was summoned to the fore. John Adams and Martin Luther King Jr., Abraham Lincoln and the signers of the Declaration of Independence, Roger Williams, Brigham Young, and Sam Adams were all made to play a role.

To his credit, Romney did attempt to address what he thought was the central issue standing between Mormons and their evangelical critics.

> There is one fundamental question about which I often am asked. What do I believe about Jesus Christ? I believe that Jesus Christ is the Son of God and the Savior of mankind. My church's beliefs about Christ may not all be the same as those of other faiths. Each religion has its own unique doctrines and history. These are not bases for criticism but rather a test of our tolerance. Religious tolerance would be a shallow principle indeed if it were reserved only for faiths with which we agree.

Yet Romney quickly moved from this briefest of doctrinal explanations to the disdain for explaining his religion that was part of his reputation.

> There are some who would have a presidential candidate describe and explain his church's distinctive doctrines. To do so would enable the very religious test the founders prohibited in the Constitution. No candidate should become the spokesman for his faith. For if he becomes president, he will need the prayers of the people of all faiths.

60

Having dismissed any need to explain his faith further, Romney returned to the far safer ground of American values and a broad American religion.

> I love the profound ceremony of the Catholic Mass, the approach-ability of God in the prayers of the evangelicals, the tenderness of spirit among the Pentecostals, the confident independence of the Lutherans, the ancient traditions of the Jews, unchanged through the ages, and the commitment to frequent prayer of the Muslims. As I travel across the country and see our towns and cities, I am always moved by the many houses of worship with their steeples, all pointing to heaven, reminding us of the source of life's blessings.

He continued in this vein for many paragraphs, to a close that invoked "the divine author of liberty" and "freedom's holy light." Long before he was done, though, he offered the words that ought to be remembered as his core message.

> Perhaps the most important question to ask a person of faith who seeks a political office is this: does he share these American values: the equality of humankind, the obligation to serve one another, and a steadfast commitment to liberty?

It was precisely because this was Romney's understanding of his task that his speech failed to hit its mark. He spoke far longer than Kennedy, using twenty-five hundred words to Kennedy's fifteen hundred. Yet he mentioned the word *Mormon* only once. He explained no Mormon doctrine aside from his brief confession of faith in Jesus Christ. He recounted nothing of the fascinating Mormon story, expressed nothing of the debt he owed to his faith, and said nothing that would deepen respect for those who shared his beliefs.

Mitt Romney is an accomplished man and an accomplished speaker. He ought to have carried the day. Yet he defined his task as John Kennedy had fifty years before. This is why he failed.

In 1960, Kennedy represented nearly forty million members of a religion that Americans largely understood. It was not ignorance of Catholicism that raised Protestant concerns. It was the possibility of Roman Catholic domination of the man in office. Kennedy answered that he was more American than Catholic and had sworn devotion to his nation.

In 2007, Romney represented only seven million American Mormons. No one worried that the Mormon Church would attempt to rule. What was in question was what Romney believed, how the teachings of his church—on race, on women, on Israel, on revelation, and even on its own historical claims—had shaped Romney's life and might shape his politics. Mormonism was not understood by most Americans, and so Romney as a Mormon was a mystery—perhaps even in the cultic sense, some believed. Men who are mysteries do not get elected president. Romney had to explain.

What he chose, instead, was to answer the question he had posed in his speech: "Does he share these American values: the equality of humankind, the obligation to serve one another, and a steadfast commitment to liberty?" Yet these topics need have nothing to do with religion, which was what voters most wanted Romney to address.

Romney chose to answer Kennedy's challenge with Kennedy's answers. *America is the land of the free. Religion does not dominate here. I am an American.* What he did not do was explain his own faith. Though this may not have been what cost him victory in 2008, as we shall see, his speech nevertheless provides an example of why the Kennedy model should no longer be our guide for religious disclosure by presidential candidates. Today we simply need something more.

★   ★   ★

We will revisit moments like these again in our future. Kennedy at Houston and Romney at College Station will return to us each time a candidate is called upon to explain what he or she believes. Kennedy and perhaps Romney will likely be invoked. History will be summoned to the stage. Promises will be made.

Yet it is not likely that future candidates will be asked to explain religions as systematic and historic as Roman Catholicism was in 1960. They will not even have to explain religions as systematic as Mormonism is now.

Instead, they will likely be required to explain faiths far more personalized, more customized, than those that have taken center stage before them. Even if they use terms like *Catholic* or *Buddhist* or *United Church of Christ*, they will—in the manner of their generation—have reworked and refashioned the faiths they attach to these labels. To explain their personal pastiche of belief, they will have to recount a bit of their journey, something of the experiences that led them to faith. They will then need to identify their principal beliefs and describe how those beliefs inform their politics.

It will not be enough simply to appeal to American values. It will not be sufficient to say that the presidential oath is safeguard enough. Americans are learning that the faiths of presidents inform the thinking of presidents, which in turn shapes the actions of presidents. The people will want to know the things they wish they had known of previous presidents. They will want to ask questions. They will expect meaningful answers.

# 2

# Test of the Fathers

Growing up in Britain as a rather loose Jew, the two things
that didn't belong together were freedom and religious
intensity. In America, they do. The Founding Fathers made
a bet that if you didn't force everyone to profess religion
in a particular way, you could protect intellectual freedom
and religion would flourish.

Simon Schama

Surprisingly, the idea of asking candidates to explain their faith
makes some Americans squirm. It seems intrusive. It seems somehow
bigoted, unfair—even un-American. This is perhaps because we feel
the impact of our history. We remember that our forefathers resisted
the idea of religious conformity and so outlawed religious tests for
public office. We somehow think that to "ask the question" about
the religion of a candidate is to erect the kind of religious barriers
the founding fathers opposed. When we press for understanding,
we feel ourselves more in the court of King George III than in the

counsel of Jefferson and Franklin. We feel ourselves undoing the wisdom of our founding, somehow betraying our heritage.

We should delve into this matter of religious tests, then, to see if we do indeed betray our past by pressing for religious clarity from our leaders. We want nothing more than to be distinctly American in this matter of religion and politics, and so we should measure ourselves against the vision of our founders. Perhaps if we are fortunate, "the end of all our exploring will be to arrive where we started and know the place for the first time."[1]

There is a moment in our early national history that has long been lauded as testament to the power of religion in our country. It has just as long been badly misunderstood. It occurred on June 28, 1787, during the Constitutional Convention in Philadelphia. We remember this as a dramatic episode in the American journey, a time when our best minds and noblest patriots were contending with the grand ideas that would define our new nation for generations to come. This may have been true, but it did not feel that way to the men gathered in that steamy room in the Pennsylvania state house on June 28, 1787.

A friend reporting events to John Adams, our ambassador in London, wrote, "Money is the only object attended to, and the only acquisition that commands respect. Patriotism is ridiculed; integrity and ability is of little consequence."[2] In a separate letter, Adams read, "We are now in State of Anarchy and Confusion bordering on Civil War."[3]

It was true. After the inspiring unity of the war years, the colonies had become states and then had quickly descended into squabbling like grasping little fiefdoms. Some states raised such high tariffs that trading with them became impossible. A few of the larger states even sent their own ambassadors abroad. Hardly a day went by when one faction or another didn't threaten to abandon the United States and become a nation of its own.

In Philadelphia, tempers flared. Alexander Hamilton had already gone home in a huff. Other delegates spoke of doing the same. In Paris, Thomas Jefferson cheered them on: "I hold it that a little rebellion now and then is a good thing . . . a medicine necessary for the sound health of government."[4]

This didn't help General Washington, Benjamin Franklin, or the other patriot leaders who were seated at green felt-covered desks in Philadelphia. It was hot enough given the summer sun. Then someone commented that the public could hear everything being said through open windows. General Washington, who presided over the meeting, ordered the windows and shutters closed. The room became stifling. Emotions sent temperatures even higher.

Just as yet another speaker was about to take his turn, eighty-one-year-old Benjamin Franklin gestured to General Washington. Dr. Franklin had something to say. This surprised everyone. The aged inventor had taken to writing down his thoughts and asking a fellow delegate to read them aloud. Now, though, he intended to speak for himself. With great effort, he used his walking stick to raise himself from his chair. The other speaker deferred. General Washington nodded. The room went uncommonly silent.

Mr. President, the small progress we have made after four or five weeks close attendance and continual reasonings with each other . . . is methinks a melancholy proof of the imperfection of the Human Understanding.

We seem to feel our own want of political wisdom, since we have been running about in search of it.

In this situation of this Assembly, groping as it were in the dark to find political truth, and scarce able to distinguish it when presented to us, how has it happened, Sir, that we have not hitherto once thought of humbly applying to the Father of lights to illuminate our understanding?

In the beginning of the Contest with Great Britain, when we were sensible of danger, we had daily prayer in this room for Divine protection.—Our prayers, Sir, were heard, and they were graciously answered. All of us who were engaged in the struggle must have observed frequent instances of a superintending Providence in our favor.

At this point, it surely dawned on more than one delegate that these were odd thoughts to come from Dr. Franklin. He was known for his rationalist views. In fact, he was famous for his religious skepticism. Yet here he was stating with certainty that God had intervened in the recent war and on behalf of the American cause. What was the old schemer up to? Perhaps noticing the questioning looks forming on faces, Franklin pressed on.

To that kind Providence we owe this happy opportunity of consulting in peace on the means of establishing our future national felicity. And have we now forgotten that powerful Friend? Or do we imagine we no longer need His assistance?

I have lived, Sir, a long time, and the longer I live, the more convincing proofs I see of this truth—that God Governs in the affairs of men. And if a sparrow cannot fall to the ground without His notice, is it probable that an empire can rise without His aid?

Dr. Franklin was far from done. Some delegates likely wondered how he could stand so long, feeble as he was. But stand he did, while he quoted scripture, rebuked the assembly for "local interests," and warned that if things kept on as they were, "we shall become a reproach and bye word down to future ages." Finally, the good doctor moved to a close.

I therefore beg leave to move—that henceforth prayers and imploring the assistance of Heaven, and its blessing on our deliberations, be held in this Assembly every morning before we proceed to business, and that one or more of the clergy of this city be requested to officiate in that service.[5]

Stunned silence followed. Jonathan Dayton, a delegate from New Jersey, recorded, "The Doctor sat down; and never did I behold a countenance at once so dignified and delighted as was that of Washington. . . . The words of the venerable Franklin fell upon our ears with a weight and authority, even greater than we may suppose an oracle to have had in a Roman senate."[6]

This is the moment the myth began. Franklin's words were so moving that generations of Americans since have been unable to envision the men in Philadelphia not being moved by them as well. Surely they rose to their feet in shouted affirmation. Surely every morning thereafter the convention began with a clergyman's prayer. Surely this was the turning point of all turning points in the history of religion in America.

Yet it was not. The delegates did not approve Dr. Franklin's proposal. They took no action at all. We might want the story to end with words like these: "From that day on they opened all the constitutional meetings with a prayer." These are the words Ronald Reagan used to tell this tale. He had heard it that way often. It just wasn't true. Practical matters loomed too large for the men in Philadelphia, some scholars suggest. They didn't want to offend Philadelphia's Quakers. They didn't want to signal the public that something was wrong. They didn't want to haggle over where to find the money for the clergyman. It just didn't happen. Dr. Franklin himself noted, "The Convention, except three or four persons, thought prayers unnecessary."[7]

In fairness, his words did have impact. As Jonathan Dayton wrote, "We assembled again and . . . every unfriendly feeling had been expelled, and a spirit of conciliation had been cultivated."[8]

On July 4, the entire convention also assembled in the Reformed Calvinistic Church to hear prayers and a sermon by Rev. William Rogers.[9] The words of Benjamin Franklin, the well-known religious skeptic, had urged the delegates to remember God in this of all times. They did.

We should not misunderstand what happened that day in Philadelphia. It is an episode that reveals much about our history. It not only illustrates one of the most important truths behind our laws and institutions but also goes far in explaining what the founding fathers intended for the vital matter of religious tests for public office. In knowing this and knowing it fully, we can understand how our founders intended for us to deal with religion in the lives of our political candidates.

The men gathered in Philadelphia in 1787 were not against religion. They were, for the most part, Christian men who were members of churches and who believed in a prayer-answering God.[10] Yet they also believed something else that surely played into their decision not to act on Franklin's proposal, something that we have a hard time envisioning today. They believed the federal government should have nothing to do with religion.

We should remember that these men had just fought a war of independence from an empire in which church and state were one. It had not served these colonists well. It had also turned the American Revolution, in part, into a war of religion. During the conflict, British troops routinely burned colonial churches to the ground. Those they didn't destroy were converted into either riding stables or houses of prostitution. Colonial pastors were often killed. Bibles and copies of the famous hymnal compiled by Isaac Watts were burned. The American colonists knew what this was. It was a state church asserting its authority over dissenters through armed troops.

Naturally, the colonists had no intention of allowing this kind of religious tyranny in their fledgling nation. They wanted decentralized authority. They wanted a very limited central government. In fact, they wanted this so much that they overdid it in their first governing document, the Articles of Confederation. By the time they arrived in Philadelphia to devise a wiser plan, they recognized the need for a tighter union, but they still did not want to make England's mistake. They did not want the federal government to have anything to do with religion. That authority would rest with the states.

This thinking guided all they did. In their minds, they were devising a federal government that had limited powers. Their job in constructing the new Constitution was to list the exact powers the federal government was to be given. If the Constitution didn't mention it, then the federal government didn't have it.

This is one reason, by the way, that they didn't get around to a Bill of Rights until much later. It was nearly an afterthought. Some of our founding fathers did not think a Bill of Rights was necessary. They believed the guarantee of freedoms for individuals came from the limited role the Constitution gave the federal government. Contain the feds, they thought, and you protect the states and individuals. That's what the Constitution did: *contain the feds*. So why should we need a Bill of Rights?

The best-known statement of this thinking came from Alexander Hamilton in *The Federalist*: "For why declare that things shall not be done which there is no power to do? Why, for instance, should it be said that the liberty of the press shall not be restrained, when no power is given by which restrictions may be imposed?"[11]

It was an issue that surfaced often when the framers presented their new Constitution to the people. Some groups or interests didn't see the issues they cared about specifically mentioned. The framers kept offering the same answer to ease these concerns. They said that if a power wasn't mentioned in the Constitution, the federal government didn't have it. Fear not.

Understandably, one of the concerns expressed by the people was the lack of a guarantee of religious freedom. When James Wilson of Pennsylvania was pressed about protections for religious rights, he replied, "I ask the honorable gentlemen, what part of this system puts it in the power of Congress to attack those rights? When there is no power to attack, it is idle to prepare the means of defense."[12] James Madison answered in much the same way: "There is not a shadow of right in the general government to intermeddle with religion."[13] Richard Dobbs Spaight of North Carolina maintained, "As to the subject of religion . . . no power is given to the general government to interfere with it at all. Any act of Congress on this subject would be a usurpation."[14]

All of this was argued well before the Bill of Rights, with its First Amendment guarantees for religion, was written. Still, the framers thought they had done for the cause of religion all that was necessary to do. They had told the federal government what its powers were. All else belonged to the people and their states. They didn't want a secular state. They wanted a nation in which the federal government had no role in religion. Let the states and the people be as religious as they want to be.

This thinking helps explain why the men at the Constitutional Convention in Philadelphia did not respond to Dr. Franklin's suggestion. They simply did not have religion on their minds. They did not make much of a connection between religion and federal doings. They were crafting a document that detailed procedures for their "general" government. They weren't writing a grand poetic statement like the Declaration of Independence.

In fact, it was boring. It was meant to be. They didn't want the federal Constitution to be sexy. They wanted the federal government to do as little as it could and then leave the people alone. This is one reason the occasional brave soul will attempt to memorize the Declaration of Independence but hardly anyone bothers to memorize the Constitution. It's a snore.

The truth is that religion was so absent from the deliberation of those men in Philadelphia that Dr. Franklin's words were one of only two times that religion was even mentioned during the convention. The other was when they decided on language to prevent religious tests.

★   ★   ★

This matter of religious tests was handled fairly quickly. On August 20, 1787, Charles Pinckney from South Carolina proposed language to be included in the new Constitution: "No religious test or qualification shall ever be annexed to any oath of office under the authority of the U.S."[15] Pinckney was concerned that while the federal government had no responsibility for religion, it could be made religious if a religious oath was required to hold a federal office.

For example, if a person needed to pass a uniquely Presbyterian test of some kind to hold an office, the government would be filled with only Presbyterians. Or at least with people willing to act like Presbyterians. This cut across the goal of having a central government that had no authority in matters of religion. Pinckney saw that religious tests could be a sneaky back door through which a religion could come to dominate the federal government. He decided to close that back door.

His proposal went to the Committee on Detail. Ten days later the Committee on Detail reported back to the convention. They had forgotten a detail, though. They had failed to mention Pinckney's language. So he proposed it again from the floor of the convention. The chairman of the Committee on Detail, perhaps embarrassed about allowing details to slip, stated that the provision was "unnecessary,

73

the prevailing liberality being a sufficient security against such tests."[16] In other words, *since we all feel so good about each other, surely something like this isn't necessary.*

Thankfully, two other delegates approved Pinckney's motion. It was immediately put to a vote. It passed. No further debate occurred.

Then it went to the Committee on Style. Yes, they actually had a Committee on Style! God knows Congress could use such a thing today! This committee reworked the language into what we now know as Article VI, clause 3, of the US Constitution: "No religious Test shall ever be required as a Qualification to any Office or public Trust under the United States."

It is with this clause that our national hesitation about questioning political candidates about religion probably begins. Our founding fathers didn't want our federal government to be religiously slanted one way or the other. So they made religious tests for public office illegal. We draw from this a feeling more than a thought: *Don't bother people about religion when they're campaigning for office.*

There are two vitally important truths about this we ought to know. First, we must remember that the founding fathers made a huge distinction between the states and the federal government that has dimmed for us today. They spoke of the "United States" and the "States" as two different things. The "United States" was the federal government. The "States" were individual entities like Virginia and Massachusetts.

Article VI, clause 3, of the Constitution addresses the "United States." To the framers, this meant only the federal government. We should remember that nothing in the Constitution applied to the states at the time it was written. This would only come decades later. In some matters, it would take more than a century for constitutional restrictions to apply to the states.

Remembering this, it should come as no surprise that all but two states that existed at the time the US Constitution was ratified had some form of religious test. All but two—Virginia and New York—had them. Only the federal government—the "United States"—was forbidden to have such tests.

These state tests took various forms, but most were intended to make sure only Protestants held office. Some went further. For example, the Massachusetts constitution required a person chosen for a public office to affirm, "I believe the Christian religion, and have a firm persuasion of its truth."[17] The Delaware constitution required a public office holder to make an even broader affirmation: "I, _____, do profess faith in God the Father, and in Jesus Christ His only Son, and the Holy Ghost, one God, blessed for evermore; and I do acknowledge the holy scriptures of the Old and New Testament to be given by divine inspiration."[18]

Again, all the states except two had some kind of religious test at the time the US Constitution was ratified. Many of these state tests were written or approved by the same men who had signed the federal Constitution banning religious tests in the "general" government. This was exactly what the founding fathers intended. They wanted a federal government with no authority in religious matters. They wanted states and individuals to be as religious as they desired to be. Thomas Jefferson said exactly this in a letter to a Presbyterian clergyman in 1809.

> I consider the government of the United States as interdicted by the Constitution from intermeddling with religious institution, their doctrines, disciplines, or exercises. This results not only from the provision that no law shall be made respecting the establishment or free exercise of religion, but from that which reserves to the States the power not delegated to the United States. Certainly, no power to prescribe any religious exercise, or to assume authority in religious

discipline, has been delegated to the General Government. It must then rest with the States, as far as it can be in any human authority.[19]

&#9733; &#9733; &#9733;

The first of the two truths we need to know about the ban on religious tests in the US Constitution is that it initially applied only to the federal government and not to the states, as we have seen. The second truth we need to know is that, despite this ban, the framers did expect candidates for public office to be examined about their religious views. They expected the people would do it. The framers not only expected this but also relied on it.

Our founding fathers were not narrow, ignorant people who knew only their relatively small, almost entirely Christian, colonial world. No, they were well-read people of the world. They understood how nations worked, and they understood the trends of their times. They knew changes would come to their new nation over time, and they knew some of those changes would be in the arena of religion.

An indication of this broad understanding is revealed in how often our founding fathers and our early national leaders contemplated non-Christian religions playing a role in American life. It was not unusual for a man like George Washington, for example, to mention "Jews, Mahomitans or otherwise" in a letter to George Mason about state support for religion.[20] When an associate asked what kind of workers to get for Mount Vernon, Washington answered, "If they are good workmen, they may be from Asia, Africa, or Europe; they may be Mahometans, Jews, Christians of any sect, or they may be Atheists."[21] So vast were the General's options. In 1786, Thomas Jefferson was proud of the fact that Virginia's Statute for Establishing Religious Freedom protected "the Jew and the Gentile, the Christian and Mahametan, the Hindoo and the Infidel."[22] Many of the founding fathers believed, as John Locke had written in his *Letter Concerning Toleration*, "Neither Pagan nor Mohometan, nor Jew, ought to be excluded from the civil rights of the commonwealth because of his religion."[23]

Chief Justice Joseph Story, the premier jurist in our early nation, best captured the founders' realization that many religions would likely play a role at the federal level when he wrote, "The Catholic and the Protestant, the Calvinist and the Arminian, the Jew and the Infidel, may sit down at the common table of the national councils without any inquisition into their faith or mode of worship."[24]

Obviously, there were many who feared this openness. When the US Constitution was being debated in state legislatures, there were loud protests over the absence of religious tests. People were afraid that without such tests non-Christians could hold office. David Caldwell, a Presbyterian minister in North Carolina, was in favor of a religious test that would eliminate "Jews and pagans of every kind."[25] A Baptist minister named Henry Abbott complained, "As there are no religious tests, pagans, deists and Mahometans might obtain office."[26]

Our purpose here is not to enter this debate. Rather, our purpose is to listen to what some of the founding fathers said in reply to one of the people's concerns. This concern amounted to a common fear at the time: *If we don't have religious tests, then people of any faith can hold federal office.* The answer of our founders was clear and consistent: *We want the people, not a simplistic religious test, to decide who is qualified for public office and who is not. The decision rests with the people.*

Consider, for example, the words of Richard Dobbs Spaight, one of the signers of the Constitution.

> As to the subject of religion . . . no power is given to the general [federal] government to interfere with it at all. . . . No sect is preferred to another. Every man has a right to worship the Supreme Being in the manner he thinks proper. No test is required. All men of equal

capacity and integrity are equally eligible to offices. . . . I do not suppose an infidel, or any such person will ever be chosen to any office unless the *people* themselves be of the same opinion.[27]

Just for the moment, we should try to step around any offense we might feel at the thinking that no infidel could ever be chosen for public office. Spaight was a product of his time, just as we are products of ours. The more important point for our purposes here is that this founding father believed we did not need religious tests. The people could be trusted to pay attention to the religious beliefs of political candidates. The people would choose according to their preferences.

Consider also the words of Supreme Court Justice James Iredell, who was appointed by George Washington and served from 1790 to 1799.

But it is objected that the people of America may perhaps choose representatives who have no religion at all, and that pagans and Mahometans may be admitted into offices. . . . But it is never to be supposed that the *people* of America will trust their dearest rights to persons who have no religion at all, or a religion materially different from their own.[28]

Again, for the moment let us step around the issue of whether a person without a religion can hold office. It was an issue at that time. It's not a pressing issue for ours. The more important issue for us is that Justice Iredell, like most of the founding fathers, believed that the people would decide about religion in the lives of political candidates. The people would pay attention. The people would evaluate. The people would vote accordingly. This was the confidence of Justice Iredell and others regarding religion in candidates' lives.

Finally, consider the words of Samuel Johnston, a member of the Continental Congress, a member of the United States Senate, and the governor of North Carolina.

It is apprehended that Jews, Mahometans, pagans, etc., may be elected to high offices under the government of the United States. Those who are Mahometans, or any others who are not professors of the Christian religion, can never be elected to the office of President or other high office, but in one of two cases. First, if the *people* of America lay aside the Christian religion altogether, it may happen. Should this unfortunately take place, the *people* will choose such men as think as they do. Another case is if any persons of such descriptions should, notwithstanding their religion, acquire the confidence and esteem of the *people* of America by their good conduct and practice of virtue, they may be chosen.[29]

This eminent statesman took the case even further. He said that while it would, in his opinion, be unfortunate should the American people elect a non-Christian to public office, they might do it if they ceased to be Christians themselves or if they found a person of a non-Christian faith to have good character and be of virtue. Remember that this is a statement in defense of outlawing federal religious tests. Clearly, Samuel Johnston placed his entire faith about such matters in the decisions of the American people. They would pay attention. They would evaluate. They would make the best choice at the time.

When Dr. Franklin urged prayer that steamy summer at the Continental Convention in Philadelphia, the delegates took no official action but did take the words to heart and did, outside of their official business, gather to give thanks, hear a sermon, and pray. It was faith exercised as a personal choice. It was faith practiced outside of federal business. It was faith as an expression of culture, of heart, and of meaningful connection to God.

This is very much what the founders intended for the role of religion in the nation. Let the people be whatever religion they might choose. Let the states do so as well. Yet give the federal or general government no role in religion. Let it not establish a religion nor prohibit the free exercise of religion—as the First Amendment would eventually say—nor be shaped by religious tests. Instead, the people will choose—as an expression of culture, of heart, and of meaningful connection to God.

The founders trusted that we would be vigilant. They trusted that the American people in each generation would take note of religion in politics and decide on the matter of candidates accordingly. Not as bigots. Not as those conspiring to make their religion prevail. Instead, the people would be vigilant because they would know the power of religion in human affairs, and they would understand its meaning as they considered what was best for the republic.

The distinction our founders made between federal and state governments has been removed through the years. The courts have read the Fourteenth Amendment as requiring that the restrictions on the national government should also apply to the states. Now the states may no longer require religious tests.

It is interesting that the last vestige of these state tests fell in a Supreme Court case named *Torcaso v. Watkins*. Maryland had a provision in its constitution requiring a person to declare belief in God to hold office. Roy Torcaso, an atheist who had been denied a job as a notary public, challenged the requirement and won. Amazingly, this case did not come before the Supreme Court until 1961, a sign in the modern era of the system set in place by our founders nearly two hundred years before.

What has not changed is the founders' expectation that the people should be the ultimate decision makers about faith in public office. There has never been a more important time for a reclaiming of this responsibility. Faith is as much a factor in the challenges of our time as ever. There are also more varieties of faith than ever. It is important that the people live out the founders' hopes.

The conclusion is that asking the important religious questions of our candidates is not un-American. It is not contrary to the thinking of the founders, nor is it something done only by the bigoted or the conspiring. It is what the founders expected and our times demand. It is also in the best interest of our nation. There should be religious tests: the test of the people, not tests imposed by government.

It is time, then, to live out the old Celtic maxim:

That which thy fathers bequeathed thee
Earn it anew if thou would'st possess it.

# 3

# Noah's Wife Was Joan of Arc

I am quite sure now that often, very often, in matters concerning religion and politics a man's reasoning powers are not above the monkey's.

Mark Twain

A humorous list has been making its way around the internet in recent years. It takes on various forms, is attributed to everyone from Ann Landers to Mark Twain, and seems to morph as it becomes ever more viral. It makes us laugh even while making us aware of a problem we face in America.

This list is comprised of answers people have given to Bible questions. We learn from it, for example, that the epistles were the wives of the apostles. Apparently, the Finkelsteins—not the Philistines—were a race of people who lived in biblical times. Lot's wife was a pillar of salt by day, but she could be a "ball of fire" at night. She may have been similar to Mary, who gave birth to Jesus because she had "an immaculate contraption."

The fifth commandment, we discover, is "Thou shalt humor thy father and thy mother." The seventh is "Thou shalt not admit adultery." This may be necessary because the apostle Paul preached "acrimony," another word for marriage. All of which explains why a Christian should have only one wife, a practice called "monotony."

The poor Jews had problems throughout their history not with troublesome Gentiles but with "unsympathetic genitals." This might have been related to the fact that Joshua led them in the battle of "Geritol." They would have been better off had they lived in the time of Noah, because his wife was Joan of Arc.

In modern times, the pope lives not in the Vatican but in the "Vacuum." Iran is the Bible of the Muslims, much as Republicans are a race of sinners mentioned in the Bible. Some people have a hard time hearing in church because the "agnostics" are bad. This makes it difficult for them to pray the Lord's Prayer, which begins, "Our Father in heaven, Howard be thy name."

Now, if you've missed this list of insightful answers to Bible questions, don't despair. You can go to YouTube and watch Jay Leno ask Bible questions of people on the streets of New York. He called this, of course, "Jaywalking."

The experience was a revelation of biblical proportions. On New York's Melrose Avenue, Leno learned that Adam and Eve lived in the Garden of Eden with their child, Candy Cain. This was possible because God made Eve by opening an apple, or maybe a cow. Things moved quickly though, because not too long after this Joseph's father gave him not a coat of many colors but a new car.

Before long a whale swallowed the prophet Pinocchio. This was around the time another whale swallowed Moby Dick. When Jesus was born, he was visited by three wise men. Their names were Nina, Pinta, and Santa Maria. They brought the baby Jesus gifts: wine and a cheese platter. Perhaps this was why he taught, "Blessed are the meek, for they shall eat."

Jesus lived fairly recently—perhaps just 400 years ago, which means he lived around the time of Columbus. He might have lived 250 years ago, just before the American Revolution. Jesus was a rabbi. Rabbis are Jewish. We can be sure of this because there was one on the TV show *Friends*. He was planning to "baptize a baby."

★ ★ ★

We laugh, and we should. Religious knowledge can be confusing, with its odd names, foreign words, and easily conflated ideas. It is good to enjoy our foibles and our follies. It helps the medicine go down.

Yet what if this fun level of confusion is where most Americans live all their lives? What if our entire nation lags far behind in the religious knowledge required to contend with the many cultures of the world? What if we do not even understand the religions in our own land? How will we fulfill the founding fathers' hope that the people of this nation will evaluate the religions of their candidates?

In addition, what if this level of uncertainty and misunderstanding plagues our country's leaders? What if, out of ignorance, they ignore the importance of religion in world affairs? As they plan a war? As they negotiate a treaty? As they interact with the leaders of other nations?

There is no end to the hand-wringing and head wagging that has occurred in recent years over American ignorance of religion. It has become a cottage industry. There is much to make us concerned. Even scholars cite Jay Leno's discovery that everyone he talked to in one of his walks could name the four Beatles but none could name the four Gospels. More scientific surveys reveal that 60 percent of Americans can't name even five of the Ten Commandments and 50 percent of high school seniors think Sodom and Gomorrah were married. Most Americans are unable to name the first book of the Bible. Even the teachings of our own denominations elude us. Most

Lutherans don't know who Martin Luther was. Most Methodists can't name a distinctive doctrine of their denomination's founder, John Wesley.[1]

Matters like these are primarily of concern to Christians. Yet all Americans, regardless of their faith, should be concerned about what we do not know about the religions of the world. A survey of high school students conducted in 2005 revealed that while 36 percent of them knew what Ramadan is, 17 percent said it is the Jewish Day of Atonement.[2] The vast majority of Americans admit they are unfamiliar with the basic teachings of Islam, Buddhism, Hinduism, and Judaism. Ask them about religious terms such as *Alawite*, *Sunni*, *Shi'ite*, *animist*, or *agnostic*, and they'll simply shrug. Yet each of these terms has been essential to understanding world news in recent years.

The conclusion is that while most Americans believe religion is important, that it ought to shape our politics, and that the United States would be better off if religion were of greater influence, the very word *religion* invokes more of a mood than any discernible content for them. While this is the pitiful state of American religious knowledge, religion is daily shaping the world in which Americans live. Politicians cite religion as a basis for their decisions. School boards contend with religious content in curricula. Religion is the primary force behind many of the international events of our time. More practically, religion conditions our approaches to the matters we say are of utmost importance to us: marriage, child rearing, character, and death.

★   ★   ★

The most disturbing results of our ignorance of religion are not found in surveys or test scores. No, the real-world results are far more severe. After September 11, 2001, when many Americans were understandably angry about Islamic extremism, our ignorance of religions went on full display. On September 15, a forty-nine-year-old Sikh gas station owner in Mesa, Arizona, was shot and killed by Frank Roque. It turned out that Roque had mistaken the Sikh—with his beard and turban—for a Muslim. Roque protested to police, "I'm a patriot and an American. I'm American. I'm a damn American."[3] And so Roque murdered Babir Singh Sodhi, who was also a patriot and an American.

The next month three teenagers in Palermo, New York, burned down Gobind Sadan, a *gurdwara* or Sikh temple. They thought it was named for Osama bin Laden. Then two men beat a Los Angeles store owner almost to death. His name was Surinder Singh Sidhi. The two geniuses who nearly killed him thought he was Osama bin Laden. It made perfect sense, apparently, for Osama bin Laden—who was then the most wanted man in the world—to be masquerading as a liquor store owner in Los Angeles. The fact that Islamic doctrine forbids the sale and consumption of alcohol didn't seem relevant. Unable to distinguish between a Sikh and a Muslim, the two men beat Sidhi to do their country a favor.[4]

On October 4, 2001, a man in Texas named Mark Stroman decided he would seek revenge for the horrors of a few weeks before. He used his .44 caliber chrome-plated pistol to murder Vasudev Patel, a Mesquite, Texas, convenience store clerk. Stroman felt justified in killing Patel because he was Middle Eastern just like the men who had hijacked American planes on 9/11. But Vasudev Patel was not a Muslim. He was a Hindu. He was not from the Middle East. He was from India. In 2011 the state of Texas put Stroman to death for his crime.[5]

It seemed the idiocy would not end in those months after 9/11. Vandals threw rocks through synagogue windows in numerous American cities, unaware of the difference between a Jewish place of worship and a mosque. A pizza deliveryman was beaten in Boston while his attackers shouted that he should go back to Iraq. Saurabh Bhalerao had never been to Iraq, though. He was a Hindu.[6] Roman Catholic nuns were mistaken for Muslim women, and a Hindu was forced to leave a JetBlue Airlines flight. A native Hawaiian Protestant pastor was thoroughly questioned after he boarded a flight home from New York. He had quietly recited the Lord's Prayer before takeoff. A stewardess was sure he was praying in Arabic and reported that he might be a threat.

★   ★   ★

We can shake our heads in disgust at such ignorance, but none of it should surprise us. Most of us know that we, too, do not know what we ought to know. We realize that in all our years of formal education, most of us were never required to take a class on the world's religions. Even those with advanced degrees have likely never had such a course. Most of what we know we acquired on our own. We've had little choice.

Though some of us might sit in religious services an hour a week, less than half of that time is devoted to teaching, and even this is usually of a light and motivational kind. Few sermons deal with the doctrines of our own faith, almost none with the beliefs of other religions in the world. Outside of worship services, a very small portion of us ever attends a systematic course at our church, our temple, or our mosque. Seldom are such courses even offered.

This failure to understand religion is not only a challenge for average Americans trying to understand and contend in a global society. It is also a serious concern for those who direct our national affairs. We have come close to disaster many times in our history because religion was either misunderstood or completely ignored.

There is a story of this kind that arises from the presidency of George W. Bush. The story was widely reported at the time it happened, but its importance may not have registered with most Americans, largely because it would have required understanding one of the world's religions.

It occurred in 2003, just two months before the US invasion of Iraq. US troops had been engaged in Afghanistan for slightly more than a year. To build unity and craft strategy, President Bush met often with Iraqi leaders during this time. It was during a meeting with three such leaders that the memorable moment took place.

The three Iraqis were in the Oval Office explaining to the president what the situation might be in Iraq after the fall of Saddam Hussein. While doing so, they mentioned in passing the two religious sects in Islam, the Sunnis and the Shi'ites. According to US ambassador Peter Galbraith, President Bush didn't understand what these two words meant. The president stopped the three men and exclaimed, "I thought the Iraqis were Muslims!" Another version has him saying, "You mean . . . they're not, you know, there, there's this difference. What is it about?"[7]

We should recall that by this time Bush had been a US president for two years, the governor of Texas, and a senior advisor to another US president, his father, who was involved extensively in Middle Eastern affairs during his administration and had been director of the CIA. The younger Bush was educated at Philips Exeter, at Harvard, and at Yale. He may indeed have been the infamous C student of his many jokes, but it does seem that he had opportunity to learn the difference between Sunni and Shi'ite. Perhaps he didn't. In this, his educational experience would be similar to that of most Americans when it comes to world religions.

What is troubling is that there is hardly a place in the world where knowing the difference between Sunni and Shi'ite is more essential than in Iraq. Just after World War I, the European powers forced non-Arab Kurds, Sunni Arabs, and Shi'ite Arabs to form a new nation with a new name: Iraq. They then installed a Sunni Arab king. A workable unity has largely proved elusive ever since. The appearance of unity was usually maintained only at the price of dictatorship and often at the expense of the non-Arab Kurds.

It is possible, then, that in 2003, the United States invaded Iraq though its commander in chief did not understand the single religious fault line that would most determine the success or failure of his strategic plan. Yet even if President Bush was able to distinguish the sects of Islam and accounts of the Oval Office meeting are false, the episode is nevertheless revealing. When rumors of the president's unfamiliarity with Islam began circulating, journalists went scurrying throughout the US government to see if other officials were equally unaware. The results were disturbing.

Just months before Bush's meeting, Jeff Stein, national security editor of the *Congressional Quarterly*, had written a *New York Times* op-ed reporting that when he asked congressional leaders about the difference between Sunni and Shi'ite, most of them weren't sure.[8] "Most American officials I've interviewed don't have a clue," Stein reported. This was still the case in 2003. When Robert S. Mueller, the director of the FBI, was asked if he could distinguish the two sects, he replied, "Not technically, no." The answers proved pretty much the same for heads of congressional intelligence committees and senior staffers at the State Department.[9]

This ignorance of Islam on the part of American officials surely helped produce many of the failures evident in Iraq today. As Ambassador Galbraith recounted in his book *The End of Iraq: How American Incompetence Created a War without End* and in numerous interviews in 2006, "You can't have a national unity government when there is no nation, no unity, and no government. Rather than trying to preserve or hold together a unified Iraq, the U.S. must accept the reality of Iraq's breakup and work with the Shiites, Kurds and Sunni Arabs to strengthen the already semi-independent regions."[10] Unfortunately, ignorance of the religious and ethnic divisions in Iraq kept US officials from crafting the wisest policies.

\* \* \*

It would be easy to focus on one administration's ignorance of one religious issue at the onset of one war. Yet we would miss the broader concern. The truth is that American foreign policy has often been hampered by ignorance of religion on the part of American officials. Stories like that of Bush and Islam are nothing new.

It does not seem a difficult lesson to master. Religion is a determining factor in human life the world over. Plans and policies that do not take it into account normally fail. The pages of world history teach this. Our own American history teaches it. The headlines of our times teach it. Yet ignoring the factor of religion or failing to understand religion fully has been an ongoing trait of the US government, particularly in the arena of foreign affairs.

During early US involvement in Southeast Asia, for example, the Kennedy administration initially supported Ngo Dinh Diem as president of South Vietnam. Diem was a strident Roman Catholic whose brother was archbishop of the city of Hue. The Diem administration brutally suppressed Buddhist dissent and flaunted its support for the Catholic Church. Buddhists rioted and pled for equal treatment. Buddhist monks set themselves aflame. US officials initially missed the importance of these tensions out of a long-standing US government bias against the importance of religion. Faith may stir a local storm, but it is rarely at the heart of world events, we have often assumed. In the case of South Vietnam, religious unrest grew to such an extent that Kennedy was finally forced to agree to a coup by Diem's generals, as well as to the assassination of Diem. Some scholars have argued that ignorance of religion in South Vietnam in general and of Buddhism in particular plagued the US war effort until its end more than a decade later.

Americans prefer to think in secular terms, both in statecraft and in the writing of our history. Our first war as a nation was not against British troops in the War of 1812, as many Americans think, but against Barbary Coast pirates in North Africa beginning in 1801.

Our statesmen at the time and our historians long afterward labored to keep religion from playing a role. Our enemies did not trouble themselves with such labors. The Rais Hudga Mahomet Salamia, captain of a ship manned by American captives, expressed the view of this war that prevails even today in much of the Islamic world. He warned his captives that they would be harshly treated "for your history and superstition in believing in a man who was crucified by the Jews, and disregarding the true doctrine of God's last and greatest Prophet Mahomet."[11]

Religion often plays a role in world events. Those who choose to see only through a secular lens usually fail to see reality. Our diplomats failed to understand the importance of religion before the start of World War II. They knew Japan was undergoing a revival of Shintoism in the 1930s. They had received reports. They didn't know what it might mean. That revival of Japan's ancient religion—with its vision of Japanese domination of the world—fueled many of the atrocities that came afterward. Meanwhile, the Japanese didn't make the same mistake. They didn't ignore religion. Their military leaders chose to attack Pearl Harbor early on a Sunday morning in part because they knew it was a time when Americans would be unprepared—when most Americans in Hawaii would be either heading to church or sleeping it off. They were right.

A similar blindness to the importance of religion caused us trouble more recently in Iraq. Some advisors—a few learned US military chaplains in particular—begged senior US commanders not to send female soldiers into Iraq's Shi'ite provinces. This seemed such a bigoted suggestion that no one with sufficient power to change course listened. When a photo of an American female sergeant subduing an Iraqi insurgent hit airwaves, many in the US military were proud. The Shi'ite world was incensed.

The photo depicted the sergeant subduing an Iraqi male. She had pinned the man facedown by putting her boot on his back. Her rifle was pointed at his head. Though the sergeant was only doing as she had been trained and doing it skillfully, she had unknowingly made a huge diplomatic mistake. The man she pinned wasn't just any Iraqi male. He was a mullah, a Muslim holy man. It was an offense for a woman to touch him. It was an offense for him to be forced to the ground. It was an offense for the bottom of anyone's foot to be placed upon him. When the photo was shown on Middle Eastern television stations, it signaled an American disregard for local religion and made US objectives in Iraq more difficult to achieve. This was, once again, because American foreign policy leaders had not factored in the matter of religion.

What we find among our leaders and permeating our nation's foreign policies grows organically from our American culture. Our ignorance and even our disregard for religion come naturally to us. They are produced by some of the factors we have already seen. The desire of our founding fathers for a federal government without authority in matters of religion has made us expect the same of other countries. It has also fashioned a lens through which we view the world. Another factor is the thinking urged by men like Comte that leads us to believe that religion is dying out as a force in the world when the opposite is true. This belief can leave us clumsy and unprepared for contending with religion as a defining force in the life of nations.

Our geographic isolation, which grants us many benefits, does not help us in this matter of religion. Until fairly recently, it was possible for an American to live his entire life and never meet a Muslim, a Buddhist, or a Hindu. Now the United States shares the multicultural experience of most of the rest of the world. Even Americans in small, rural towns are likely to have neighbors from foreign countries or of different ethnicities and religions than their own. This is recent, though, and our years of isolation kept us from knowing much about the religions of the world. Most Americans still feel the same about the need for knowing world religions as they do about the need for learning a foreign language: the knowledge might be nice for its own sake, but it isn't an essential requirement for their daily lives.

All of this has come to shape what we teach in our schools, and here is where we find both the largest part of the problem and the best chance for a solution. The US Department of Education requires each state to set educational standards and determine means of testing for every subject taught from kindergarten through the end of high school. The states are helped in this task by the work of national educational associations made up of experts and scholars who provide standards and guidelines in every subject a school might teach. Religion is not a required subject, though. It is embedded in a number of disciplines, like English and social studies. It does not stand on its own in the curriculum. In a very few schools, forward-thinking teachers and administrators do sometimes offer elective courses on religious themes.

This means that students in most US schools will study religion only to the extent that it is necessary to fulfill objectives for other subjects. For example, rather than study Islam as part of a semester or yearlong course on the world's religions, students learn a bit about Islam by way of learning about the Middle Ages, the Crusades, World War I, or perhaps current events. They might also touch on Islam in studying Shakespeare's *Othello* or Mark Twain's *Innocents Abroad*. A modern literature class might require Khaled Hosseini's *The Kite Runner* or Salman Rushdie's *The Satanic Verses*. A teacher of these courses would explain Islam only as far as necessary for students to understand the references to it in these books.

By making religion a side topic within other subjects of the curriculum, educators inadvertently create an opportunity for religion to be almost entirely overlooked. Often there are no specific objectives for the religious content of a course. This means that while there might be objectives for a seventh grader's knowledge of the Crusades, there might be no objectives for the knowledge of Islam that is essential to understanding the Crusades.

In addition, making religion a side topic within other fields increases the likelihood that teachers will have had little training for teaching the religious content of their courses. They know Shakespeare but not Islam. They know about the American experience in World War I but nothing about Islam, the fall of the Ottoman Empire, or the Sykes-Picot Agreement—all of which are relevant to the situation in the Middle East today. In Florida, for example, the lengthy requirements for teacher certification in the social sciences, grades 6 through 12, include only one line related to religion: "Identify major world religions and ideologies."[12] This is overly broad and disconnected from the specifics of the curriculum. There is also no requirement for a teacher to have completed any instruction in religion in order to fulfill this single objective.

★ ★ ★

The larger problem, though, is a general hesitation about religion in public school curricula as a whole. There have been so many lawsuits and so many conflicting interpretations of court rulings affecting the teaching of religion in public schools that teachers and administrators are often confused. Joseph Laycock, professor of history at Texas State University, has written that what standards for instruction in religion do exist are often downplayed because of a "general ignorance about Constitutional law."

> Before I was a professor, I was a high school teacher. I found that teachers and administrators, as well as students and parents, had a vague sense that religion is *verboten* in public school but could not accurately articulate why. Many people seemed to believe that religion

cannot be discussed in the classroom because "it might make someone uncomfortable." This is a dangerous myth.[13]

The truth is that even the American Civil Liberties Union (ACLU)—much feared by school districts nationwide—encourages the teaching of religion as an academic subject. In its document entitled "Religion in the Public Schools: A Joint Statement of Current Law," the ACLU goes so far as to quote part of a US Supreme Court ruling, the first sentence of which ought to serve as a vision statement for the teaching of religion nationwide. It is an affirmation of religion in school curricula the Supreme Court has repeated often.

> It might well be said that one's education is not complete without a study of comparative religion, or the history of religion and its relationship to the advancement of civilization. It certainly may be said that the Bible is worthy of study for its literary and historic qualities. Nothing we have said here indicates that such study of the Bible or of religion, when presented objectively as part of a secular program of education, may not be effected consistently with the First Amendment.[14]

The ACLU's expansion on this statement is helpful and far broader than many school administrators would imagine.

> The history of religion, comparative religion, the Bible (or other scripture) as literature (either as a separate course or within some other existing course), are all permissible public school subjects. It is both permissible and desirable to teach objectively about the role of religion in the history of the United States and other countries. One can teach that the Pilgrims came to this country with a particular religious vision, that Catholics and others have been subject to persecution or that many of those participating in the abolitionist, women's suffrage and civil rights movements had religious motivations.[15]

96

School districts have overrestricted themselves, then, out of confusion about the law and fear of litigation. This has not served their students well. At a time when world events press religious questions upon them and in a generation exhibiting unprecedented religious openness, students are being denied the benefits of instruction in religion and often because their administrators and teachers are simply misinformed.

★　★　★

Students in colleges and universities suffer the same absence of teaching in religion but not because of First Amendment myths. As with public primary and secondary schools, there are no external requirements that students learn about religion as part of the general education requirements for an undergraduate degree except, again, as part of the study of other topics. Most American university students earn their degrees without ever having taken a course on the world's major religions. They will learn what they do about religions only by way of learning about literature, social science, history, and perhaps philosophy. Most of these students will have the option of taking elective courses on religion, but, never having had the value of religious knowledge urged upon them, few of them do.

It is theoretically possible, then, for American students to earn advanced degrees having never systematically studied religion beyond the briefest of mentions in courses on nonreligious topics. Aspiring lawyers can complete law school and pass the bar exam without ever having learned about the world's religions—not even to the minimal extent of explaining the religious underpinnings of their field. Medical doctors, social workers, public school teachers, accountants, engineers, historians, broadcasters, and even aspiring politicians who major in political science need not know anything about religion to acquire certifications or degrees in their field.

Hopefully, American educators are rethinking this glaring deficiency. Reconsideration is certainly happening in other leading nations of the world. In Germany, for example, education in religion is required in all schools. At the more advanced levels, this instruction is woven into the field of medical ethics and used to disarm Islamic terrorism in the minds of students.[16] Russian president Vladimir Putin signed a bill in 2012 that made religious education mandatory for all schools in the country.[17] Canada also requires its Ethics and Religious Culture (ERC) program to be taught nationwide, except in private religious schools, which are free to teach their own religion courses according to a recent Canadian Supreme Court ruling.[18] Even officially secular countries are undergoing change. In Brazil, for example, the election of Assembly of God pastor Marco Feliciano to that country's Commission on Human Rights in 2013 has brought a renewed emphasis to religious studies in the nation's schools. Now nearly half of all Brazilian schools offer some form of religious instruction.[19]

In August 2013, US Secretary of State John Kerry offered some remarks at the launch of the Office of Faith-Based Community Initiatives in Washington, DC. After a few broad statements about the role of religion in the world, Kerry came to a reflective moment. He then said, "If I went back to college today, I think I would probably major in comparative religion, because that's how integrated it is in everything that we are working on and deciding and think about in life today."[20]

Now, Kerry's education was far from deficient. He majored in political science at Yale and then completed law school at Boston College. By August 7, 2013, he had been secretary of state for barely six months. Already he had seen, though, the importance of religion in the affairs of the world and the value of the knowledge of religion to the conduct of American government.

Kerry is not alone in this conclusion. Many are realizing that we do not live in the world Comte predicted. We live in a world that is increasingly religious, that is marred by escalating religious conflict, and that demands understanding of religion from those who would seek to lead. Already a number of university religion departments have put Kerry's words on their websites. For the faculties of these departments, the words form a kind of challenge: dare to view the world through the lens of religion thus to know it more fully.

The broader challenge concerning the matter of American religion and politics is determining not only what our political candidates believe but also whether they know what they need to know about religion before they enter office. Another US secretary of state, Henry Kissinger, once described the importance of what statesmen know before they enter office.

> Any statesman is in part the prisoner of necessity. He is confronted with an environment he did not create, and is shaped by a personal history he can no longer change. It is an illusion to believe that leaders gain in profundity while they gain experience. As I have said, the convictions that leaders have formed before reaching high office are the intellectual capital they will consume as long as they continue in office. There is little time for leaders to reflect. They are locked in an endless battle in which the urgent constantly gains on the important. The public life of every political figure is a continual struggle to rescue an element of choice from the pressure of circumstance.[21]

Kissinger's observation heightens the importance of assessing the religious knowledge of political candidates. We do not want religious tests for public office in the United States because we do not want to force political candidates to comply with narrow religious standards in order to serve. It would be nice, though, to be able to give our candidates religious tests of the other kind—the kind designed to measure what they know about the religions of the world.

The solution is to encourage a religious dialogue sophisticated and open enough to tell us what we need to know about political candidates' religious beliefs and knowledge. It is true that once in office presidents are served by experts who augment their knowledge in every field. Yet, as Kissinger has said, presidents also consume their own intellectual capital. They bring their religious understanding into office just as they bring their religious faith. Voters should know what both of these are. Campaigns should be times of religious openness. There should be no mysteries and few surprises. Voting for a president ought not be a gamble, at least not in matters that can be confirmed in advance.

There is no noble cause in the United States that is not well served by a better understanding of religion. It serves the cause of national unity. It serves the cause of commerce abroad. It serves the cause of just and compassionate immigration. It serves the cause of, as the US Supreme Court has said, advancing civilization. It even serves the cause of clarity in one's individual faith.

Perhaps as important, knowing religion as we should in America will elevate our politics and help us to be wise and discerning in our increasingly faith-based world.

# PROFILE

## RELIGION, POLITICS, AND THE MEDIA

If we were to do the Second Coming of Christ in color for a full hour, there would be a considerable number of stations which would decline to carry it on the grounds that a Western or a quiz show would be more profitable.

Edward R. Murrow, *CBS News*

I am sensitive to the value of faith and religion and spirituality in people's lives because I'm a journalist.

Peter Jennings, *ABC News*

The managing editor called me in and said, "Uh—your dad's a preacher. Right?" And I said, "Yeah." And he said, "You're the new religion editor." And I was like 20 years old. I didn't know what to say, except, "Okay."

Bruce Buursma, *Chicago Tribune*

Religion often looms just behind the headlines, is often just beneath the surface of what gets reported. That doesn't mean reporters know how to talk about it. So religion rarely gets its due in world affairs.

Dan Rather, *CBS News*

Religion is a determining element in the human story, a powerful ingredient of the social mix. To disregard religion in chronicling that story prevents any intelligent perspective on conditions in this society or any other. Certainly no one can understand America, its history and present forces, without understanding the nature and history of its religious life. After all, that was mainly what brought settlers here in the first place.

George Cornell, *Associated Press*

There is irony in the fact that two great societal institutions, religion and the news media, each protected by the same constitutional amendment and each committed in its own way to serving the public, are so at odds.

John Seigenthaler, *USA Today*

Americans will respect your beliefs if you just keep them private.

Bill O'Reilly, *FOX News*

Perhaps there is an unwritten tradition of deference in the news business that keeps us out of the deep waters of faith, doctrine and spirituality. The better explanation may be that as "realists" and "empiricists" we look on religion as we look on love and hate— too much a part of us and the world to ignore but too elusive to explore.

Richard Harwood, *Washington Post*

Any contemplative tendencies that manage to survive in the media environment are largely engulfed by the pursuit of conflict. It is no accident that when Catholicism, theology and religion in general receive coverage in the press, some sort of real or perceived conflict is at the heart of the matter.

Cullen Murphy, *Atlantic Monthly*

When journalists reduce religion to politics, they tend to favor the dissidents, reformers and underdogs who engage their own political sympathies. The result is a picture that is not only one-sided but also one-dimensional. It is a tale filled with the sound and fury of partisan struggle but emptied of its spiritual significance. Reporters need not be believers to get religious stories right, but a nation of believers deserves better of its religious news.

S. Robert Lichter, George Washington University

We have this idea in our minds that there's this separation of church and state in America, which I think is a good thing. And we extend that to our politics—not just church and state, but it's also that there's a separation of religion and politics. But of course there isn't.

Stephen Colbert, *The Colbert Report*

Politics is difficult to cover objectively because we have several parties with blurred lines of distinction. Religious reporting is a hundredfold more difficult for the same reason, and because it is such an emotional issue for most people. It takes as much specialized knowledge as science and medical reporting.

Doug Mendenhall, *Decatur Daily*

We don't send someone who doesn't understand baseball to report on a game. Yet we constantly send ignorant or unskilled reporters to cover complicated religion stories. No wonder the clergy are frightened.

Gayda Hollnagel, *La Crosse Tribune*

# 4

# Three Words

A typical vice of American politics is the avoidance of saying anything real on real issues.

Theodore Roosevelt

We have seen an important truth in the previous chapter. Our founding fathers banned religious tests as a prerequisite for federal office. Instead, they put their faith in the American people, whom they trusted would always take care to examine the religions of their candidates.

Since this is true, we should consider how these examinations ought to be done. There is no better place to begin than with the presidential campaign of Mitt Romney in 2012. This is because Romney was unique among recent presidential nominees. He was devoted to a religion of systematic doctrine and clear behavioral standards. He knew what he believed, and he lived accordingly. Most other recent presidential nominees have been famously unclear, as we will see. This allows us to explore the tensions between his campaign and his faith and to witness the challenge of religious clarity in the life of a presidential candidate.

\* \* \*

By the time Mitt Romney became the Republican nominee for president in 2012, he was among the most interesting and accomplished men of his generation. It was hard to find a man with a more defining family heritage, with a greater devotion to serving others, with as much success in business, or with broader leadership experience. That he did not become president of the United States was as much a surprise to him as it was to the many pollsters and journalists who predicted a Romney win in 2012.

He certainly seemed destined for greatness. His father was the president of American Motor Company, the governor of Michigan, and a cabinet secretary in the Nixon administration. His mother was an exceptional woman who ran unsuccessfully for the US Senate in 1970. He was named for the founder of the Marriott hotel empire. His ancestors helped pioneer the Mormon Church.

He graduated from Harvard Law School and immediately launched into a storied business career that made him an immensely wealthy man. During these years, he served his church in a variety of leadership positions, which involved him in tasks as diverse as tending to the needs of Southeast Asian converts in Boston and answering anti-Mormon slurs. He was devoted. He sacrificed. While still in college, he had served as a missionary in France. He would remember it as the hardest time of his life and yet as preparation for all the success that came afterward.

He had big dreams. He ran for the US Senate in 1994 but lost that race to Ted Kennedy. He thought his political life might be over. In time, he was asked to rescue the scandal-ridden 2002 Winter Olympics in Salt Lake City. By many accounts, they were the best Olympics in the nation's history. Romney received much of the credit. His methods were celebrated. Harvard University's business school created a course devoted entirely to studying Romney's "turnaround leadership." His political fortunes soon revived. He was elected governor of Massachusetts soon after. He served in this office until 2007, ran unsuccessfully for president in 2008, and won the Republican nomination in 2012.

He was movie star handsome with a beautiful, accomplished wife and stellar children. He spoke French, read widely, and could be warm and engaging personally. On a flight from Nashville, Tennessee, after a visit to Vanderbilt University, he began talking to his fellow travelers. "Federal regulations are strangling us," he declared to those seated around him. "There is a laboratory at Vanderbilt that uses rats for experiments. There are more federal regulations for the treatment of those rats than there are for the students. They call the lab 'The Rats Carlton.' Now, that's ridiculous."[1] His listeners erupted in knowing laughter. It was a classic Mitt Romney moment, revealing a few of the gifts that had allowed him to achieve so magnificently.

Yet as evenhanded and reassuring as Romney could be, he was often off balance when it came to his faith. He was not ashamed of being a Mormon, but he did not like being questioned about it and resented it being thrown in among the swirling controversies of a political campaign.

He had declared himself truthfully in his Kennedy-esque speech at the Bush library in 2007. Ask a candidate whether he shares American values. Ask him about the equality of humankind. Probe him for a sense of his obligation to serve others. Determine whether he has a steadfast commitment to liberty. But do not ask him about his faith. It is frowned upon, both by custom and by the Constitution. It is a transgression. In this, Romney's thinking was similar to that of many other Americans who found it offensive to question a candidate about religion.

His resentment hurt him. Just before election day in 2007, he had angrily told a radio interviewer, "I'm not running as a Mormon, and I get a little tired of coming on a show like yours and having it be all about Mormons." When the questions kept coming, Romney fired back, "I don't like coming on the air and having you go after my church. I'm not running to talk about Mormonism."[2] The in-studio interview was captured on video and went viral the next day, just as Americans were heading to the voting booth.

In an interview with ABC's George Stephanopoulos during the 2012 campaign, Romney testily fielded a question about the Mormon view of the return of Jesus: "Well, I'm not a spokesman for my church. I'm not running for pastor-in-chief. I'm running for commander-in-chief. So the best place to go for my church's doctrines would be my church."[3]

This was a disingenuous answer from an otherwise thoughtful man, and the attitude that produced it played a damaging role in what was perhaps the most important speech of his life. On August 30, 2012, Romney accepted his party's nomination for president at the Republican National Convention in Tampa, Florida. It was, as all convention acceptance speeches are, an opportunity for the candidate to present himself before a national audience, to deal with any perceptions that might become obstacles on the road to the White House.

He knew that his Mormonism was just such an issue. Questions about his faith had dogged his every step to the convention, as they would in the national campaign to come. He had even complained about this to his family. In a Netflix documentary entitled *Mitt*, which was filmed during the 2012 campaign but not released until 2013, Romney spoke of the "Mormon flip-flopper" tag his critics had tied around his neck. He was finding it nearly insurmountable and knew it could mean defeat.

The convention speech was Romney's opportunity to destroy this Mormon problem. He did not take it. Instead, of the more than forty-one hundred words of the most important speech of his life thus far, he devoted only three to his faith: "We were Mormons." That was it. Three words.

Gallup reported that the speech polled lower than any other presidential nomination acceptance speech in the history of Gallup polls.[4] This was not merely because Romney refused to delve into his faith. The speech had other flaws. Religion was also not the only reason Romney lost the national election to Barack Obama later that year. That occurred largely because American crises at home and abroad better served the incumbent.

Yet a 2012 American National Election Study concluded that one in twenty Republicans stayed home and refused to vote because they did not consider Mormonism to be Christian. If all of these had voted for Romney, he would still have lost by two million votes, with 49 percent of the vote to Obama's 51 percent.[5] It would have been a much closer race, though, and it is possible that other electoral benefits might have come from Romney being more engaging about his faith. He might have won the deciding two million votes to his cause.

This leads to one of the more fascinating questions about Romney's Mormonism in the 2012 campaign and about the broader role of religion in American politics as well. What good might have come to the Romney campaign had he been willing to air his faith more openly? Indeed, what good might have come to Mormonism and to the country as a whole?

We should ponder the way Romney might have presented his Mormonism to the nation that decisive night. He knew some things about his faith that could have proven appealing to his audience had he been willing to say more than three words. One of them was that

Mormonism is a uniquely American religion. It is a religion that seems almost designed to promote patriotism, political leadership, and prosperity. Its doctrines rivet the faithful to the American experience. Mormons teach that the US Constitution was "established" by God and that the country plays a central role in divine purposes for the world.[6]

Some scholars have even argued that the Book of Mormon is best understood as an allegory of the American experience. In its pages, the faithful sail west in ships to settle where dark-skinned natives oppose them. Democratic elections are held in a New World described as "the land of liberty." This religious connection to the United States has helped make American Mormons into super-patriots. It is not surprising that the Mormon Tabernacle Choir has sung at the inaugurations of five presidents and that graduates of Brigham Young University are eagerly pursued by every branch of the US government, the CIA and FBI in particular.

Mormons are also fierce advocates of free markets. As one of their own economists has written, "Mormonism is the Protestant ethic on steroids."[7] This arises from both their history and their doctrines. They suspect overreaching government, value volunteerism, despise debt, celebrate "hard" money, admire thrift, and are religiously devoted to storing goods for a future day of trouble. Always, they believe in progress, both economic and spiritual. Brigham Young University is becoming the Harvard of libertarian economics, and Mormons now run some of the nation's largest corporations.

Mormon constitutional scholars, jurists, and historians have been among the most influential in the nation. Not only do most Mormons consider the Constitution to have been revealed by God, but they also see in its words guarantees of the freedoms and the opportunities to prosper that they so prize. When Glenn Beck warns his audiences that the nation is straying from its constitutional roots, it is Mormon scholars he quotes. When the most popular homeschool curricula teach students about an "original intent" approach to interpreting the Constitution, Mormon books and study guides are likely involved. Almost alone among American religious denominations, the Mormons have clung to the Constitution as an essential part of God's will for the nation.

Romney might have extolled these features of his faith that night in Tampa. It would have helped to defuse his Mormon problem. He could have won voters who were suspicious of him previously and could have ended the evening having convinced large numbers of Americans to take him seriously as the best man for the job.

★　　★　　★

It also would have helped had he been willing to describe his people's sufferings. Few outside of the Mormon fold know that the Church of Jesus Christ of Latter-Day Saints is the only religion in American history ever targeted by an extermination order. It occurred in 1838 and was known as Missouri Executive Order 44. It issued from the pen of Governor Lilburn Boggs and made a chilling demand: "The Mormons must be treated as enemies, and must be exterminated or driven from the State if necessary." The order was not rescinded until 1976.

This and other forms of persecution drove the Mormons west in what Mormons today remember as "the Great Trek." Six hundred died in the first winter of this forced migration. Hundreds more died from the cold or starvation soon after while pulling handcarts through mountains and snow to reach Salt Lake City. Dozens died at the hands of mobs. A young girl who witnessed a murderous scene was haunted for the rest of her life by the memory of dead bodies falling to the bottom of an unfinished well. It is a memory that also lives in Mormon minds today.

Those sufferings were not remote to Romney. They had befallen his own family. He had also faced hardships like them himself.

His great-great-grandfather Parley Pratt, a Mormon Church founder, was murdered for his faith in 1857. His great-grandparents were driven out of the United States to Mexico by religious persecution and returned when forced to by the start of the Mexican Revolution in 1910. Romney's father remembered all his life the sound of gunfire and of rebels walking through village streets. He later said, "We were the first displaced persons of the 20th century."[8]

Mitt Romney faced something of this same animosity toward his faith years later. When he was a regional church leader in Belmont, Massachusetts, from 1981 to 1986, a fire destroyed the Belmont meetinghouse. Authorities concluded the fire was intentionally set. Arson certainly wasn't a new weapon in the arsenal of Mormon hatred. Mormon meetinghouses had been burned down for a century and a half by the time of the Belmont fire. Fortunately, Romney was able to arrange meeting space for the congregation with a variety of other churches. He then paid for much of the rebuilt facility himself.

We can imagine what invoking Mormon patriotism and Mormon struggles might have meant at the Republican National Convention of 2012. Romney's Mormonism was, aside from his business and political experience, the most prominent feature of his life. Nearly everyone watching that night knew of it. Many voters were still undecided about it. Even a large percentage of Republicans were yet unsure. Few would have known much of the Mormon story, its Americanism, or the role that Romney's family played. It deserved more than three words. Identifying himself more fully with his deeply American faith and its sufferings—and being careful not to neglect its astonishing successes and achievements—would have served Romney, the Republican cause, and perhaps the American religious dialogue well.

Suppose he had offered a brief moment in that all-important speech that went something like this: *Though I am a son of privilege,*

*I am also the son of a persecuted religion. I have known bigotry, much as my ancestors did before me. I am a Mormon, and while I admit it is a religion out of the mainstream, I also declare that it is a religion that has moved me to love my country, my wife, my children, hard work, clean living, and the cause of serving the hurting and the poor. I do not ask America to embrace my Mormon faith. I do ask America to embrace a man my faith has helped to produce, a man who cherishes the freedom of all Americans to worship as they choose. My fellow Americans, let us—whatever our faith—serve this nation and make her better. This is what my faith calls me to do. It is also what I hope to do as your president.*

A single paragraph similar to this one would have cost Romney 150 words in a 4,100-word speech. They might have made all the difference. Had he exhibited this openness throughout his campaign, it might have transformed his image. Think of how the hurting, the poor, the victims of religious bigotry, and the lovers of religious liberty might have been drawn to him. Think of how such a relaxed, humble, courageous approach might have endeared him to uncertain voters nationwide. Given that his opponents endlessly portrayed him as a heartless, greedy corporate raider, airing his religion truthfully might have changed the outcome of the election.

Yet Romney limited himself to those three words because he believed what he had said in his "Faith in America" speech in 2007.

> There are some who would have a presidential candidate describe and explain his church's distinctive doctrines. To do so would enable the very religious test the founders prohibited in the Constitution. No candidate should become the spokesman for his faith.

What Romney did not appreciate was that no one wanted him to speak for his church or to all of its doctrines. What they wanted was to understand how Mormonism affected him—its virtues, its troubles, and, yes, its theological distinctives. He was right that Americans do not send a candidate's church to the White House. They do send the candidate's religion, however, because it is always with the candidate who is religiously sincere. This is what Romney did not understand and why the wall of separation he attempted to erect between candidate and faith hampered his cause.

This case was solidly made a week after the 2012 election by Kathryn Lofton, professor of American studies and religious studies at Yale University. In an article entitled "Mormonism Cost Romney the Election (But It's Not What You Think)," Lofton suggested that while Obama had transformed his "itinerant childhood and complicated genealogy into something profoundly relatable," Romney had not done the same for his Mormonism.

> In the end, the most potent secret is the one advertised, but not revealed. And Romney's mistake has been to avoid explaining the most open secret of his leadership, namely just how Mormon he is. He ought to have unveiled the relationship between his particular religious sensibility and his ideas for American success. He should have announced at every pit stop that he had met the world through his missionary work; that he came from a good Christian home that emphasized the principles of hard work and self-sacrifice; that he keeps a weekly calendar guided by the principles of Stephen R. Covey; and keeps a marriage because he believes those commercials are right—diamonds are forever, and so is this bond. He should have proclaimed his financial success was the result of all this earnestness, and explained private equity as just another way to organize free enterprise. Not because it's a crafty re-framing of his biography, but because it is also true: it's true to the very thing his supporters find so solid, and his detractors find so discomfiting, about Romney.[9]

According to this view, Romney did not lose because he was a Mormon. He lost, in part, because he was not willing to be Mormon enough.

★   ★   ★

There is, of course, another side of the Romney Mormon issue, and it has to do with the obligations of the media and voters to explore a candidate's faith as far as it is relevant to his conduct in office. In 2012, it was not only Mitt Romney who was obligated to air his beliefs so far as they were relevant to his hopes of governing. The voters and the media had an obligation too. They had a duty to press for answers about Romney's Mormonism until they could envision how it would shape him in the Oval Office. This kind of questioning need not take on the tone of a witch hunt. It ought not become merely a tool of political opposition. It should be, though, a part of the people's vetting process for any presidential candidate who is sincere about a religion.

Romney's Mormonism carried with it a number of features that voters ought to have known about and that journalists ought to have explored once he declared his intentions to be president. Some journalists did, and their work was valuable. Most didn't, and this was part of a general hesitation about religion that besets American media.

It is understandable. To speak negatively about a person's religion raises questions of motive, possible bigotry, and even basic truthfulness that are sometimes hard to answer. Still, this is the job of the media in a democracy, and it can be done thoroughly and yet kindly and honorably.

Certainly, part of this thorough but well-intentioned approach involves focusing mainly on those features of religion that relate to the task of governing. Every religion includes beliefs that seem strange to outsiders. They merit investigation in the life of a political candidate only if they relate to governing. For example, most Christians believe in a resurrection, most Muslims believe in the prophetic gifts of Muhammad, most Buddhists believe in the enlightenment of

Siddhartha Gautama, and most Hindus believe in a concept of the physical universe called *maya*. Few outside these faiths would agree with what those inside these faiths believe. Since these articles of faith do not directly relate to political leadership, journalists should treat them only in passing. To do otherwise tends toward bigotry and persecution.

★   ★   ★

An example of this in Mitt Romney's life and faith is the Mormon history of polygamy, or "plural marriage." Romney himself has by every account been faithful to one wife all his life and fiercely argues that polygamy is no longer part of his church. He is right. Yet polygamy is so woven into his family history and the Mormon story that it looms large for those newly exposed to his faith.

Joseph Smith, the prophetic figure whose revelations became the main teachings of Mormonism, claimed to have received revelations about polygamy long after he had founded the Church of Jesus Christ of Latter-Day Saints. His Book of Mormon says nothing about it and instead urges monogamy. It wasn't until more than ten years after the start of the faith that Smith made public his new thinking about plural marriage. It appears in one of the official Mormon books called *Doctrine and Covenants*.

> And again, as pertaining to the law of the priesthood—if any man espouse a virgin, and desire to espouse another, and the first give her consent, and if he espouse the second, and they are virgins, and have vowed to no other man, then is he justified; he cannot commit adultery for they are given unto him; for he cannot commit adultery with that that belongeth unto him and to no one else.
>
> And if he have ten virgins given unto him by this law, he cannot commit adultery, for they belong to him, and they are given unto him; therefore is he justified.[10]

This was highly controversial, even among the Mormons. Brigham Young, Joseph Smith's successor, was devastated by the news: "It was the first time in my life that I desired the grave, and I could hardly get over it for a long time. And when I saw a funeral, I felt to envy the corpse its situation."[11]

Nevertheless, Mormons embraced this new practice as the will of their heavenly Father and as a prerequisite for "celestial exaltation." They were vilified for it, murdered for it, and driven from their homes for it time and again.

Finally, in 1890, Mormon president Wilford Woodruff declared polygamy at an end. He said he had received a revelation from his heavenly Father. Critics charged that he had also received a revelation from the US Congress, which had banned polygamy in 1882 and would not recognize Utah for statehood as long as the practice continued. The US Supreme Court upheld the ban in 1890, creating a crisis for church leaders.

Some Mormons refused to accept this change to God's plan. They continued practicing plural marriage and endured criminal prosecution by the US government—prosecution often assisted by the larger body of non-polygamous Mormons. Many of the dissidents left the country.

This brings us back to the Romney story, which is tightly bound to polygamy. Parley Pratt, the Romney ancestor who was murdered for his Mormonism in 1857, is often celebrated as a martyr of the Mormon faith. Yet he was shot by the estranged husband of his twelfth wife. This makes his death no less tragic, but it does change our perceptions of the man. Romney's great-grandparents fled to Mexico because they were among the dissident Mormons who continued practicing plural marriage after 1890. It is the reason Romney's father was born there and vividly remembered scenes from the Mexican Revolution.

Like most members of his faith, Romney sees the Mormon years of polygamy as a God-ordained season of testing and purification. It is easy to understand why the subject disturbs him. Critics often speak of polygamy as a central feature of his faith, as though somehow he should be held responsible for it. The truth is that the practice ended in his family a generation before him and ended in the main body of his church more than half a century before he was born. Still, polygamy looms too large in the Mormon story for Romney to escape the topic as long as he continues in public life.

★   ★   ★

A more valid question regarding Romney's faith pertains to the nearly 150-year ban of blacks from the Mormon priesthood. In Mormonism, every male can be a priest, so a ban from the priesthood is nearly a ban from the faith as a whole. Romney was a leader in the church while this ban was in place. For some critics, this was not unlike being a voting member of the Ku Klux Klan.

This ban is one of the most disturbing aspects of Mormonism, largely because it means that the religion absorbed unaltered some of the most disturbing aspects of American society in the early 1800s. It began in the summer of 1835 when Joseph Smith welcomed a visitor to the Mormon enclave. His name was Michael Chandler, a peddler and showman. He had been touring the United States with four Egyptian mummies and some Egyptian documents, or papyri. Chandler had heard that Smith knew something about ancient languages and hoped he would be willing to do a translation.

The truth was Smith knew little about ancient languages, ancient Egyptian in particular. He was known for "translating" the golden plates that became the Book of Mormon. He had stated publicly that they were written in "Reformed Egyptian." Yet he did not translate in any traditional sense. For Smith, translating meant receiving revelations about what was written on the plates. Of course, non-Mormons doubt that these golden plates ever existed. Moreover, scholars have never heard of Reformed Egyptian outside of Mormon teaching. Yet this experience is what gave Joseph Smith something of a reputation for languages.

With the help of other Mormons, Smith purchased Chandler's Egyptian wares. Soon after, he proclaimed them the writings of Abraham. They were accompanied by the writings of Joseph from Egypt. Then came the translation, done in the same way Smith had translated the Book of Mormon: by revelation.

Mormonism had already answered the question of who American Indians were. They were the lost tribes of Israel, Smith had confirmed. Now, he turned to the question of blacks. He was convinced with most others of his time that all races descended from the sons of Noah: Ham, Shem, and Japheth. Noah had cursed his son Ham, declaring that he would be a "servant of servants" to his brothers. And Ham, of course, was black. Nearly everyone accepted this as a fact of history in Smith's day.

In his translation of Abraham's work, Smith took this theory even further. He recalled the biblical picture of the heavenly battle between God and Lucifer and made it an explanation for dark skin. Apparently, those heavenly spirits who held sympathy for Lucifer's cause were cursed and cast down from heaven. As founding Mormon elder Orson Hyde expounded, these spirits "rather lent an influence to the devil, thinking he had a little the best way to govern, but did not take a very active part, anyway were required to come into the world and take bodies in the accursed lineage of Canaan; and hence the negro or African race."[12]

Smith was doing little more than placing a divine stamp of approval on the racism of that time. For more than 130 years, Mormons would teach that black skin was a sign of a curse from God. This strengthened the institution of slavery and lent support to nearly every form of racism we find disgusting in our history today.

Typically, Smith was ever the contradiction. He sometimes encouraged abolitionism. There were even a few black Mormons who served as priests. Yet the racist doctrine he divined out of a peddler's parchments institutionalized racism in the Mormon Church. Brigham Young built on this and gave it the ferocity that marked his approach to doctrine. In Young's view, the only way a man could atone for marrying a black woman was to chop off his own head, spilling "his blood upon the ground."

Mormon doctrine changed in 1978. LDS president Spencer W. Kimball, claiming a series of revelations, declared, "All worthy male members of the Church may be ordained to the priesthood without regard for race or color."[13] This change did not come about as fruit of repentance or regret for past racism. Instead, God had spoken. A new day had dawned. Mormons believed that if God had not changed his mind about race, he had at least changed his manner of dealing with the faithful. Mormon apostle Bruce R. McConkie made this quite clear a few months after the decision: "It doesn't make a particle of difference what anybody ever said about the negro matter before the first day of June of this year, 1978."[14]

In the popular Broadway play *The Book of Mormon*, a character named Elder Kevin Price, a missionary, cheerily sings, "I believe that in 1978 God changed his mind about black people."[15] This is quite literally what Mormons believe. The relevant question, though, is what did Mitt Romney believe and what does he believe now?

By 1978, Romney had graduated from the Mormon West Point, Brigham Young University. He had served as a Mormon missionary in France. He was, by that year, a lay clergyman and counselor to the president of the Boston Stake. He was also thirty-one years old—mature enough to form his own opinions. Obviously, his opinions were Mormon. What does this mean about Romney and race? What would it mean in the Oval Office? These are legitimate questions of the type that ought to be asked of one running for president of the United States.

★   ★   ★

This matter of race, Romney, and Mormonism raises another question of the kind that legitimately ought to be asked of presidential candidates. Mormons are devoted to prophecy and revelation. They believe God speaks and that he speaks not just of global and church matters but of personal matters like marriage, children, and vocation. It is a belief that voters would need to understand of a Mormon running for president.

Kathleen Flake, a Mormon and a professor at Vanderbilt University, has said, "Joseph Smith was the Henry Ford of revelation. He wanted every home to have one, and the revelation he had in mind was the revelation he'd had, which was seeing God."[16] It is hard to overstate what this has meant to Mormonism. The entire religion is built on a belief in an open heaven, on the certainty that God speaks, speaks often, and speaks about anything he wishes and that his words are to be diligently obeyed.

Joseph Smith was devoted to supernatural events nearly from his birth. He and his father were known as diviners who could discern by supernatural means the location of water or which path a lost calf had taken. As a young man, Smith commanded a widespread reputation for such phenomena. Even a Mormon historian has admitted as much: "Now, most historians, Mormon or not, who work with the sources, accept as fact Joseph Smith's career as village magician. Too many of his closest friends and family admitted as much, and some of Joseph's own revelations support the contention."[17]

Mormons believe Smith's early mysticism was an untutored phase of the righteous supernatural flow that would come afterward. Critics see it as evidence he was a nut. Whatever the case, in time nearly every truth of Mormonism would come by supernatural means.

The religion was born in Smith's claims of visitations by heavenly beings. He would report appearances by God the Father, Jesus Christ,

John the Baptist, Moses, Elias, and Elijah. Angels visited regularly. They gave information about golden plates. Smith translated the plates by supernatural means and started his church when a revelation came during a worship service. His ongoing revelations created the church's doctrines. As one historian wrote of this time, "Revelations came like water from an inexhaustible spring."[18]

What is important to know for modern purposes is how this early experience shaped LDS beliefs about the nature of revelation. For Mormons, no revelation is final. All revelation is, to use their term, "progressive revelation." A common church saying is, "A living prophet trumps a dead prophet." In other words, revelations past may at any time be replaced by new revelations. The truth is always being given. It was not given once and for all long ago.

This belief has shaped the Mormon experience profoundly. It is fruit of their history. Ten years after the founding of the faith, the prophet Joseph Smith announced that God wanted men to marry multiple wives. It was part of the path to exaltation in the afterlife. His followers obeyed. This continued for decades. Mormons were killed and imprisoned for this practice. Many of them. Then suddenly, in 1890, it was over. Polygamy was forbidden. It was a sin. God had spoken.

Blacks were once understood as being black because of a curse from God. Indeed, they were made for slavery. They were made to serve the servants of their white brothers. A century and a half of this horror went by. Then, in 1978, it all ended. Blacks were suddenly allowed to enter the priesthood. No questions need be asked. No searching of the past need ensue. God had spoken.

This is the way of Mormonism. Yet these prophetic rulings do not just apply to the major doctrines of the church. They also apply to personal matters. Mormons believe that God gives direction to leaders for the good of the led. These revelations are given in temple rituals no "Gentile"—non-Mormon—may see. They are given as guidance for the young, to missionaries regarding where they should serve, to Brigham Young University graduates about their life's work. Young mothers ask elders about how many children they should have. They will have already asked for revelations about whom they should marry. They will ask about other matters time and again.

What does this mean for Mormons in politics? Suppose a voter casts his ballot for a Mormon candidate because of his position on same-sex marriage. It is possible that while that candidate is in office, his church's position could change regarding same-sex marriage. This would not be a policy decision based on consensus and research. It would be because God has spoken.

Nor is this an imaginary possibility. There have already been changes in Mormon thinking about homosexuality. Not long ago gays were routinely excommunicated from the Mormon fold. Now they are referred to as the "same-sex attracted." They are allowed to assume a place in the church and to work for its good as long as they remain celibate. Will further change occur? Almost certainly. In fact, it has already begun. In 2012, the church recognized what it once called an "abomination" as a deeply ingrained condition that "should not be viewed as a disease."[19]

This is the same revelatory progression Mormons have made in other matters. In the matter of same-sex marriage, they are already open to a redefinition from their heavenly Father. Though their official position paper on polygamy affirms traditional marriage— "Marriage between one man and one woman is God's standard for marriage"—it concludes with these words: "unless he [God] declares otherwise, which he did through his prophet, Joseph Smith."[20]

For Mormons, no revelation is final. Everything can change. This may be fine for those within the faith, but those non-Mormons who vote for Mormon politicians may need more definite assurances. This is not bigotry. It is not a veiled form of religious spite. It is merely the need of voters in a democracy to know which values a candidate plans to represent.

It is helpful to use Mitt Romney's story as a vehicle for exploring religion in the lives of presidential candidates. Romney has had his moment and is now settling comfortably into the role of Republican elder statesman. He will likely not run for president again, nor is he likely to take offense. He has certainly heard it all before. His experience, though, has much to teach.

Yet the important question is not about Romney. It is about whether Americans will become wiser in exploring the religious lives of candidates. Will we politely but firmly ask the questions we need to ask? Will we recognize that the same religion that shapes the candidate can shape his policies and through them define vast portions of our national life? Will we also become more sophisticated in our understanding of religion so that we can know which religions might lead to midstream changes in a candidate's views?

We celebrate the diversity of religions we have in the United States, and we celebrate the freedoms each religion enjoys. This comes with a responsibility, though. We must also know what these religions contend and what it will mean when one of their faithful assumes political power. It is what being an American today demands.

# 5

# Thomas Jefferson Was a None

In the United States, the majority undertakes to supply a multitude of ready-made opinions for the use of individuals, who are thus relieved from the necessity of forming opinions of their own.

Alexis de Tocqueville

There was a phrase that Winston Churchill's friends often used of him. They meant it kindly, though with a hint of British sarcasm. He was always throwing himself into new causes. Some new field of knowledge or some herculean endeavor would capture him, and he would plunge in for weeks at a time with the excitement of a child. He would inevitably end up in such a stir that he would forget there were people there before him. More than one expert grew cross when Churchill spoke as though his brilliant ideas—sometimes minutes old—had never before occurred to humankind.

When Churchill was at it again, his friends would turn to each other in their droll, upper-crust English manner and say something like, "How's Churchill? Oh, you know how it is. He's just discovered the poor." This was the phrase they used when Churchill was a rising politician searching for solutions to poverty. Years later someone asked about him and was told, "Yes, Churchill. Well. Well. He's just discovered the Navy." Not too long after that the standard comment was, "The Prime Minister? Oh, he's just discovered America."[1] And so it would go. Everything was fresh and thrilling to Churchill. Sometimes he forgot he was not the first to think the things he did.

This Churchill factor happens often when new ideas come on the scene. There is excitement. The brilliance and shine enthrall. We like to believe there has been nothing like it before. We convince ourselves that our generation is the first to think a thought or the first to see things in a certain light. We love to see ourselves as the pioneers, the first adventurers to plant a flag or the first to make a discovery in the lab. This is fine in technical fields. New discoveries happen all the time, and often they are thrilling. With cultural trends, though, we are usually just experiencing our generation's version of something that has already been. This is because history turns in cycles and human nature doesn't change much, which is what moved Harry Truman to say, "The only thing new in the world is the history you don't know."[2] It is also why King Solomon wrote, "There is nothing new under the sun."[3]

This need for perspective, this need for cooler heads and humbler hearts, comes to mind when we watch the growing fascination in our day with the phenomenon of religious "nones." It is the term we now use for those who say they don't fit any of the traditional religious categories. When filling out a form that asks them to name their religion, they simply check "none of the above." It means that none of the words commonly used to indicate faith—the name of a Christian denomination, the name of another world religion, or the terms *atheist* or *agnostic*—proved a good fit.

The initial excitement surrounding this new term was as though someone had landed on Mars. Immediately, people who pay attention to such things began claiming that this was the term of the future. America was becoming a nation of nones. It meant religion was passing away in the United States, the Christian religion in particular. An article in the *Huffington Post* claimed the "nones" are now the "dones"—as in done with religion—which means "the present church you can kiss goodbye."[4] There have been a thousand predictions along these lines, most of them amounting to a breathless resurrection of Comte.

These overheated predictions aside, the nones are indeed an important group to consider. They will likely impact every area of American society, politics in particular. They will run for public office, shape markets, and influence the direction of culture. Overreaction to them will also be a factor. Pundits are already using the rise of the nones as evidence that religion will be banished from the earth. This belief could cause Americans to pay even less attention to the influence of religion in the world and not more as our times demand.

No one is more surprised by the stir attending the nones than the man who first coined the term. His name is Barry Kosmin. He is a professor of public policy and law at Trinity College in Hartford, Connecticut, and the director of the Institute for the Study of Secularism in Society and Culture. He has also helped conduct the American Religious Identification Survey since its inception in the 1990s. It seems that years ago he became uncomfortable with labeling people "other" in the survey work he did. He tried terms such as *nonreligious*, *nonaffiliated*, and *non-faith*. They weren't accurate enough. Just because a person wasn't part of a religious institution didn't mean he or she had no faith or religion. "Nomenclature is quite important in these things," Kosmin said. So he began using the word *nones*, short for "none of the above." Kosmin didn't think the word would catch on. "It was a joke," he says, "but now, like many of these things, it has taken on its own life."[5]

Kosmin's joke caught on because of the staggering statistic behind it. In a comprehensive 2015 Religious Landscape Study, the Pew Research Center reported that 23 percent of the US adult population considered themselves nones. This was a sharp increase from the 16 percent of Americans who had claimed that category in 2007. During the same period—from 2007 to 2015—the number of people identifying themselves as Christians fell from 78 percent to 71 percent.[6] The obvious conclusion is that Americans are leaving traditional religions in increasing numbers and either doing religion on their own or not doing religion at all.

This 23 percent is a significant number. For perspective, we should recall that 25 percent of Americans are evangelical Christians, and 21 percent of Americans are Roman Catholic. This means that there are now more nones in the United States than there are Roman Catholics and almost as many as there are evangelical Christians. These are now the three largest faith categories in the United States. It also means that there are now approximately as many nones in America as there are people who think the sun rotates around the earth, who want their state to secede from the union, and who believe that aliens have come to our planet.[7] Just for perspective.

There is no denying the trend, though. Nones are a rapidly growing and deeply influential force. This is, first, because they are young. They will shape the future. They comprise 35 percent of the Americans born from 1981 to 1996. Their average age is now thirty-six, and that number is likely to drop. It was thirty-eight in 2007. Nones are also increasing with stunning speed. For the number of people in that category to rise from 16 percent of Americans to 23 percent in nine years is astonishing. Population changes tend to occur slowly. This one isn't. The nones will be a defining force in the United States for years to come.[8]

★　★　★

Yet we should be careful about drawing ironclad conclusions about nones. The category is simply too broad and ill defined to support overly specific predictions or to allow us to be precise. The truth is that a none is simply a person who does not fit a predefined religious category on a form. This is the only fact that is true of all nones. Beyond this, the category splinters.

A small portion of nones are atheists (13 percent). Some are agnostics (17 percent). Nearly 30 percent of nones say that religion is important to them. About 39 percent say that religion is not very important to them, though they may "do" religion from time to time. Overall, 69 percent of nones report that when it comes to religion, they are simply "nothing in particular."[9]

What broad conclusions can we possibly draw from numbers like these? Do nones believe in God or don't they? Do they go to a place of worship regularly or not? Have they migrated from faith to no faith, from having a religion to abandoning belief? Do they practice a faith of any kind? We simply cannot answer these questions given the wide religious diversity of the people we call nones. We can be sure they exist. We can be sure they will increase in number. We know they will have a huge impact on American society and in arenas as diverse as book buying and voting. But who are they exactly? We simply cannot know with certainty.

The term *nones* is so broad, in fact, that it can include people who are active in a church if that church is not part of a denomination. Religious trends expert Ed Stetzer contends that the influence of denominations is declining, but this is not necessarily a sign of a decline in the influence of religion. He reports, for example, that the membership of the Southern Baptist Convention has declined every year for the last decade. Yet evangelical Christianity—which includes Southern Baptists—has grown 1.5 percent in the same period.[10]

This is possible because the trend in evangelical Christianity is toward large, independent churches—which means churches that are not part of a denomination. It is a trend that includes churches like the twenty-five-thousand-strong Willow Creek Community Church outside of Chicago and the thirty-thousand-member Church of the Highlands in Birmingham, Alabama—neither of which is part of a denomination. This means that, technically, the faithful, active members of churches like these are nones. It also confirms that the word *nones* is too broad to be useful.

Not only is this new concept too broad for the kind of predictions some experts are making, but it also isn't new. We may have heard of nones only recently. Experts may have "just discovered" nones in the way that Churchill "discovered" new causes, but the nones by one name or another have long been with us.

A none-type dynamic occurs whenever people living in a free society—a society that allows them to make their own religious choices—find that their faith no longer fits the old categories. We are more aware of it as a statistical phenomenon today because we are more aware of statistics. Yet it has occurred often in history, particularly in American history.

Ironically, some of the denominations that exist today began as none movements. They started as a gathering of believers who looked at the religions around them and found all of them wanting. They refused to identify themselves with any denomination or, in some cases, even to use the word *denomination*. This was certainly the case with the movement we know as the Churches of Christ today. It was also true of the Church of Jesus Christ of Latter-Day Saints—the Mormons—which was created based on the belief that all denominations had gone astray and that the righteous should avoid them completely. Both of these religions, and others like them, were at least for a season made up of people we would today call nones.

* * *

We can also be certain that nones aren't entirely new because some of the most famous Americans have been nones. Thomas Jefferson fits this category. His religious life became so nontraditional that historians have fought over it for years. Schools of thought have nearly become armed camps. Professors have been fired for their views on the man. In one famous case, a publisher pulled its book about Jefferson's faith from bookstore shelves, so great was the firestorm of controversy surrounding it. Thomas Jefferson's religious views simply did not fit traditional categories, which makes him a helpful symbol of what is coming our way, particularly in American politics.

Jefferson was born in Albemarle County, Virginia, in 1743. This was a time, says one historian, when a "vital religious culture" prevailed and "no less than some 60 percent of the adult white population attended church regularly."[11] Jefferson's early years were spent entirely within the Anglican tradition. He was baptized as an infant in an Anglican church. He attended Anglican services at Fredericksville parish throughout his youth. He completed his formal studies at the College of William and Mary, then an Anglican school. In 1767, he became a vestryman in his parish. This required that he "conform to the doctrine and discipline of the Church of England."[12] These words form the banner over the first phase of Jefferson's religious life.

In 1768, he became a member of the Virginia House of Burgesses. He was typical of the Anglican farmer/aristocrat of his day. He regularly attended his Anglican church, supported Christian causes and clergymen, participated in the religious rituals that came with being in government, and sprinkled his correspondence with references to prayer, providence, and "Almighty God."

During the revolutionary period, he authored the American creed. He wrote the first draft of the Declaration of Independence and exalted "the laws of nature and nature's God" and "sacred" rights "endowed" by the "Creator." He also wrote the original draft of the Virginia Statute for Establishing Religious Freedom. In this he declared, "Almighty God hath created the mind free." It meant that "all men shall be free to profess, and by argument to maintain, their opinions in matters of religion, and that the same shall in no wise diminish, enlarge, or affect their civil capacities."[13] In his 1781 *Notes on Virginia*, he asked the enduring question, "And can the liberties of a nation be thought secure when we have removed their only firm basis, a conviction in the minds of the people that these liberties are the gift of God."[14] Some historians have suggested that Thomas Jefferson wrote the nation into being. It was nearly true.

While he was serving as ambassador to France, he visited his friend John Adams in London and attended a Unitarian church. This was in March 1786. In May, he wrote to a friend, "I . . . seek my religion out of the dictates of my own reason, and feelings of my own heart."[15] This may have seemed a slight change in tone from his earlier, more traditional days of faith, but it would come to prevail over time.

Two years after this a friend asked Jefferson if he would sponsor his child in baptism. Jefferson declined.

> The person who becomes sponsor for a child, according to the ritual of the church in which I was educated, makes a solemn profession, before God and the world, of faith in articles, which I had never sense enough to comprehend, and it has always appeared to me that comprehension must precede assent. The difficulty of reconciling the ideas of Unity and Trinity, have, from a very early part of my life, excluded me from the office of sponsorship . . . the church requires— faith. Accept therefore Sir this conscientious excuse.[16]

Clearly, he was rethinking his faith. This was occasioned in part by his disgust for the French clergy. He wrote George Washington in 1788 about "priests and nobles combining together against the people" and to another friend that "the clergy and nobility, as clergy and nobility eternally will, are opposed to giving . . . representation [to the people] as may dismount them from their back."[17]

This disgust festered during his years as secretary of state and vice president. He read the books of freethinkers who criticized Christianity and fed on the teaching of the Unitarian Church. The offense he took with the clergy deepened. In 1798, he wrote James Madison that the New England states "are so priest-ridden, that nothing is to be expected from them, but the most bigoted passive obedience."[18] His offense turned to anger, which distanced him from his church and its doctrines.

Suspicions about his religious views began to swirl, and this occurred just before his presidential campaign in 1800. He endured relentless bombardment for being a rationalist. A New York Presbyterian named William Linn wrote an essay entitled "Serious Considerations on the Election of a President." Linn accused Jefferson of "disbelief of the Holy Scriptures . . . rejection of the Christian Religion and open profession of Deism."[19] Other essays like it began circulating. Most were guesswork. Jefferson had said little publicly about his religious doubts, so his critics were left to trade in conjecture and lies. Still, there was some truth to their views. Jefferson had stepped away from traditional Christianity.

He won that election, of course, but not until thirty-six ballots had been cast in the House of Representatives. It had been a bitter, bruising, exhausting experience, the painful imprint of which never left him. It did not help that he continued to confound both his critics and his friends in matters of religion.

In his inaugural address in 1801, he spoke of "acknowledging and adoring an overruling Providence." He had no quarrel with God or his rule of the world. He despised the religious systems devised by men. A few days after his inauguration he wrote to a friend in New England, "[In] your part of the Union . . . the temples of religion and justice, have all been prostituted there to toll us back to the times when we burnt witches." The clergy, he wrote, "twist its text till they cover the divine morality of its author with mysteries, and require a priesthood to explain them."[20] Clearly, he continued to revere God while despising much that was built in his name.

Still, he managed to keep his balance. He kept up friendships with clergymen of every kind, encouraged and attended worship services in the new Capitol building, and gave money to support religious causes. Always he was eager to preserve the purity of religion by keeping it from state intrusion.

Yet he could not see his way to declare a day of prayer and fasting as president because he believed it tended toward an "alliance between Church and State."[21] He had famously written the Baptists of Danbury, Connecticut, that he understood the First Amendment to erect a "wall of separation between Church and State."[22] These words were his personal opinion. They would become the law of the land in 1947.

Still, he was fierce in condemning the clergy. As he wrote to his attorney general Levi Lincoln, "From the clergy I expect no mercy. They crucified their Savior who preached that their kingdom was not of this world, and all who practice on that precept must expect the extreme of their wrath. The laws of the present day withhold their hands from blood. But lies and slander still remain to them."[23]

He also grew to distrust that the Bible had been preserved without corruption. He honored God, admired Jesus, and thought the scriptures offered "the purest morality ever taught to mankind."[24] Yet he believed that much of what passed for God's truth in the Bible wasn't.

He wrote a *Syllabus of an Estimate of the Doctrines of Jesus Compared with Those of Others* and introduced it to Benjamin Rush by saying, "To the corruptions of Christianity I am indeed opposed; but not to the genuine precepts of Jesus himself: I am a Christian, in the only sense in which he wished any one to be; sincerely attached to his doctrines, in preference to all others; ascribing to himself every *human* excellence; and believing he never claimed any other."[25] This was where his reading and offense had carried him. He no longer believed in the Trinity, thought Jesus was an admirable man but certainly not God, and yearned for a religion untroubled by spiritual mysteries and the silly priests who devised them: "We should all then, like the Quakers, live without an order of priests, moralize for ourselves, follow the oracle of conscience, and say nothing about what no man can understand, nor therefore believe . . . the Platonic mysticism that three are one, and one is three."[26]

He had come far from his days as an orthodox Anglican. He wanted a reasonable faith. Simplicity became his measure of truth. "The sum of all religion," he wrote, "as expressed by its best preacher [is] 'fear God and love thy neighbor.'" This he could embrace because it "contains no mystery, needs no explanation."[27]

He did not cease to confound friend and foe alike in the last years of his life. He spoke of Presbyterian clergy as his "enemies" and as "the most intolerant & tyrannical of all our sects."[28] He thought every young man living in his day would die a Unitarian. He even referred to himself as a Unitarian. Yet he attended and financially supported the Episcopal Church. He came to the conclusion that the New Testament's book of Revelation was not inspired by God, but he took comfort in the Psalms and the Gospels. He openly attributed success in the Revolutionary War to "providence" but thought reason the only reliable guide to life. As he lay dying, he quoted the Gospel of Luke—"Lord, now lettest thou thy servant depart in peace"—and then said, "I now resign my soul, without fear, to my God."[29]

★  ★  ★

Thomas Jefferson was a none. Like the nones we know today, he was offended by arrogant, misbehaving clergy and by what we now call "organized religion." He said if a truth wasn't reasonable, he could not believe it, so he discarded doctrines he once affirmed, the Trinity, the inspiration of some books of the Bible, and the divinity of Jesus among them. He also pondered other religious systems. He read the Koran, investigated the occult, and was intrigued by Native American religions. He simplified. He boiled down, reduced to a minimum, discarded the complex. He came to a faith that was at the least comprised of belief in God, love of the Bible, devotion to the example of Jesus, an obligation to "love thy neighbor," and the call to use wealth to do good in the world. He worshiped God in a dozen different churches and also helped organize religious services in "the Hall," as he called it: the US Capitol building.

He was a none before Kosmin coined the term. He was also one of our most religious presidents. He studied theology, talked of it constantly with friends, and read the Bible through again and again, often in the original languages. He had dozens of friendships with clergymen and was ever asking his friends about their faith, ever eager to hear of a new book or religious idea. He was a man seeking God but suspicious of religious organizations. He was a man who loved people but knew that when people got religious, it sometimes made them weird. He searched for truth wherever that search took him, even when it took him outside traditional boundaries.

He was also opinionated, too quick to draw conclusions, brilliant, talented, and fascinated with everything from the organs of cattle to the ways of the stars. He could be immoral, arrogant, hypocritical, and vain. He was the best of us. He was just like us. He was strange.

Thomas Jefferson was a none. Returning to our purposes in these pages, his position as a none meant you had to ask questions to find out what he believed and how he would lead. He defied the categories and changed quickly. You had to pay attention.

★   ★   ★

Abraham Lincoln was also a none. In fact, he may have been more a none than Jefferson. He never joined a church, never clearly stated what he believed about Jesus, never lost his suspicion of certain types of preachers, and always wished that churches made more sense, made fewer demands, and would simplify their complex theological systems. He also shared a major belief of the nones today: religion should be measured by the good it does in the world.

Lincoln had a hard life, and it made his journey to faith hard-won as well. He grew up in a time of wild frontier revivals. His parents were enamored with them. Abraham never was. This may have been because his father was the kind of man who would weep about Jesus over dinner and then beat his son for laziness the next day. The two grew to despise each other. Abraham didn't attend his father's funeral and didn't name his son after him, which was the tradition at the time. In fact, Abraham Lincoln felt so abused by his father that he told his audiences years later that he had once been a slave. It was something he shouldn't have said when people with black skin were in chains being worked into the grave, but it helps us understand the agony of his early years.

His father's abuse tortured him. So did grief. He lost his mother when he was nine, his sister when he was sixteen, and the first love of his life when he was in his early twenties. He told a friend he was haunted by the thought of rain falling on graves. His early grief and his innate sensitivity exposed him to bouts of depression. More than once in his life friends stood suicide watch to keep him from ending the pain.

When he was finally on his own, he moved to New Salem, Illinois. He was hungry to learn and escape the life of a laborer. He read widely, enlisted tutors, and spoke of becoming an exceptional man. His voracious program of self-education led him to the writings of religious skeptics like Thomas Paine, Robert Burns, Edward Gibbon, and Volney. He drank deeply of their disdain and then fell in among a group of antireligion freethinkers in New Salem. A friend wrote in later years, "In 1834 . . . he was surrounded by a class of people exceedingly liberal in matters of religion. Volney's 'Ruins' and Paine's 'Age of Reason' passed from hand to hand and furnished food for the evening's discussion in the tavern and village store. Lincoln read both these books and thus assimilated them into his own being."[30]

He became the village atheist. He carried a Bible only to argue against it and roamed the streets looking for someone to debate. He even wrote a booklet called "Infidelity," in which he declared his newfound spite for religion. A friend who knew he had political ambitions threw the thing in a fire. This enraged Lincoln, but the friend understood that you couldn't write a booklet "against Christianity, striving to prove that the Bible was not inspired and therefore not God's revelation, and that Jesus Christ was not the son of God," and ever get elected to a public office.[31]

Lincoln was known for being contentious about religion but also for his sadness. A man who knew him at the time said, "Now does not melancholy drip from this poor man?"[32] In the journals of friends, he was often compared to Job. Still, he was elected to the state legislature, and this required a move to Springfield. The Lincoln of this time has been perfectly captured by the novelist Thomas Keneally.

> So here is Lincoln in the spring of 1837: tortured in equal and abundant measure by self-doubt and ambition, ill-clothed, rough mannered, hard up, possessed of his peculiarly American powers of articulation and charm, burdened by what now would be considered clinical depression, plagued by exultant vision, yearning for and terrified by women, raucous in joke telling, gifted in speech, abstinent in drink,

profligate in dreams. No man ever entered Springfield, a town that would become his shrine, as tentative, odd-seeming, and daunted as Abraham Lincoln.[33]

In Springfield, he would rise on the strength of his gifts. In time, he would wed Mary Todd, have children, open a law practice, and begin to gain a reputation for intelligence, courage, and wit. He would also soften on religion—a bit. In Springfield, he met well-educated Christians who could offer explanations for their faith that the simpler folks in New Salem hadn't known. He also met clergymen he respected who impressed him more than the sweaty, shouting, bombastic ones he had seen on the frontier. In 1846, after he had lived in Springfield slightly more than a dozen years, a woman asked him about his religion. He gave her an answer that concluded with these words.

> I cannot without mental reservations assent to long and complicated creeds and catechisms. If the church would ask simply for assent to the Savior's statements of the substance of the law: "Thou shalt love the Lord thy God with all thy heart, and with all thy soul, and with all thy mind, and thy neighbor as thyself," that church would I gladly unite with.[34]

He sounds like Jefferson. For Lincoln, these words signaled a world of change. He believed in a God, spoke of Jesus as the Savior, and said there was a type of church he would join—if it existed. We also know he had friends among the clergy, gave money to Christian causes, and even loaned his horse and buggy to the new Baptist preacher in town for more than a year. Still, he wouldn't join a church. He was irritated by the narrowness of churches. He was, as he said in his answer to the woman who inquired of him, despairing of creeds and catechisms. Like Jefferson, he wanted a simple, understandable religion built on a few high-minded principles.

Clearly, there had been a change. Tragedy would carry him further. His beloved son Eddie died horribly of tuberculosis in 1850, and Lincoln sank into depression. His wife howled hysterically through the night like a wounded animal. A local minister stepped in, helped Abraham through it, and worked to deepen his faith in God. It seemed that spiritual growth came only on wings of sorrow in Lincoln's life.

He had already served in Congress by this time. Throughout most of the next decade he practiced law. He also gave some fine and well-timed speeches that brought him to national attention. His fame grew. In 1860, he surveyed the scene and knew the moment had come. He had dreamed of the presidency since childhood. Now, he decided to run. It was a bruising, faith-based campaign of the kind we know today, but he won. He became, then, the president of a union just then dissolving and seemingly destined for war.

On the train from Springfield to Washington, the burden of it nearly overwhelmed him. Each time the train stopped, Lincoln gave speeches that revealed God was much on his mind. In Lafayette, Indiana, he said, "I trust in Christianity, civilization, patriotism."[35] In Cincinnati, he invoked "the Providence of God, who has never deserted us."[36] He intended to turn, he told Columbus, Ohio, "to the American people and to that God who has never forsaken them."[37] "I must trust in that Supreme Being," he said in Buffalo, New York, "who has never forsaken this favored land, through the instrumentality of this great and intelligent people. Without that assistance I shall surely fail. With it I cannot fail."[38]

He would preside over a nation intent upon blood. The hatred of brothers, new technologies, and the follies that reign on battlefields made his war among the goriest in history. He felt it keenly and was known for walking the White House in the night like a restless ghost, groaning for the lives lost and enslaved.

He tried to stop it. He did his best in his first inaugural address. It ended with a heartrending plea: "In your hands, my dissatisfied fellow countrymen, and not in mine, is the momentous issue of civil war. The government will not assail you. You can have no conflict, without being yourselves the aggressors. You have no oath registered in Heaven to destroy the government, while I shall have the most solemn one to 'preserve, protect and defend.'" He concluded with poetry that will never be forgotten.

> I am loathe to close. We are not enemies, but friends. We must not be enemies. Though passion may have strained, it must not break our bonds of affections. The mystic chords of memory, stretching from every battlefield, and patriot grave, to every living heart and hearth-stone, all over this broad land, will yet swell the chorus of the Union, when again touched, as surely they will be, by the better angels of our nature.[39]

He did what he could, spoke of what he knew, but he could not have known what would come. He learned he was not in control. No man was. The war seemed to take on a life of its own. Armies wouldn't fight when ordered, the best generals often couldn't win, and even nature seemed at times a combatant. An otherworldly force seemed to rule. Lincoln did as he could but far too often was forced to watch in resignation as things went wrong. He said often, "I claim not to have controlled events, but confess plainly that events have controlled me."[40]

This brings us to his second inaugural address. It is one of the greatest speeches in history but at its heart is complete resignation before providence. Only four years have passed since the first inaugural address, but Lincoln has traveled lifetimes in his perceptions of God. He had said in his first inaugural address that the coming war was in the hands of the South. He would never say such a thing now. These four years later he understands. Now he accepts what he could not before.

> The Almighty has His own purposes. . . . If we shall suppose that American Slavery is one of those offences, which, in the providence of God, must needs come, but which having continued through His

appointed time, He now wills to remove, and that He gives to both North and South, this terrible war, as the woe due to those by whom the offence came, shall we discern any departure from those divine attributes which believers in a Living God always ascribe to Him?[41]

This was Lincoln's view of God in 1865, just weeks before John Wilkes Booth's derringer ball entered his brain at Ford's Theater. *There is a God. He rules. He is just. He will visit a war on enslaving people. Let us acknowledge it. Then let us heal.*

He did not think the speech would live on. He thought it fell flat. The reason? "Men are not flattered by being shown that there has been a difference of purpose between the Almighty and them," he explained to a friend.[42]

This was the end of Lincoln's journey of faith. He had begun as an embittered child in the home of a bruising father. He had suffered too much grief and had turned it all to hatred toward God. Then he mellowed when he began living among wiser heads in Springfield. When his son died, he reached for help and a Presbyterian minister stepped in. It made a difference. Lincoln afterward believed in God but wrestled with his purposes. He never understood. He could acknowledge these purposes, though, and speak of them to the country. In the last great speech of his life, he thought he was telling the nation of the great chasm between themselves and the Almighty.

He died just after speaking to his wife of his longing to see Jerusalem. He had never joined a church. He had never written a definitive theological statement. He had never been baptized. He despised the way some theologians defended slavery. He despised the way clergymen were often so sure. He read his Bible. He prayed. He buried yet another son while in the White House. Always, he was haunted by rain falling on graves.

He was ever in spiritual progression. He changed, grew, and learned. Those nearest to him had to pay attention. On any day he might step miles from where he had been the day before. At a cabinet meeting in 1862, he suddenly announced he had made a covenant with God and intended to issue an Emancipation Proclamation: "I made a solemn vow before God, that if General Lee was driven back from Pennsylvania, I would crown the result by the declaration of freedom to the slaves."[43] This startled the cabinet, changed the nation, and elevated Lincoln to Great Emancipator. It was all fruit of his ever-evolving search for God.

Lincoln was like Jefferson. He was an early version of the nones. Spiritual but not religious. Enamored with God but not with human systems. Open to scripture but insisting it pass the test of reason. Awed by God's works but unsure of his purpose. Yet both men understood their nation and their political task as ordained by the same "Benevolent Being."

The nones are not new. They've always been with us. We just didn't have the statistics or a category they could call their own. It shouldn't surprise us that two of our most spiritual presidents, if handed a form asking about their religion, would very likely have checked "none of the above."

Harry Truman was right: "The only thing new in the world is the history you don't know."[44] Our nation will be shaped by the phenomenon of the nones. It will transform our politics too. Already the millennials are voting in nontraditional ways—conservative on some issues, liberal on others. They are the main body of the nones, so this is not likely to end soon. Still, we need not wonder what a growing tribe of "spiritual but not religious" voters and candidates will be like. We've already seen them reflected in the lives of two of our nation's greatest men. Perhaps more like them is nothing to fear.

We will have to ask questions, though. We will have to pay attention. This is the price we pay for democracy, for believing that all should have access to our corridors of power.

# PROFILE

## MILESTONES IN AMERICAN RELIGION AND POLITICS

**June 15, 1215** English noblemen compel King John to recognize individual rights in the Magna Carta. This lays a basis for the Declaration of Independence and the Bill of Rights.

**June 7, 1628** The *Petition of Right* arises from English legal reforms. It establishes rights and liberties for the common man and influences the thinking of the American founding fathers.

**1630** John Winthrop, a Puritan layman, gives his "A Model of Christian Charity" sermon aboard the ship *Arbella* while en route to the New World. In the sermon, he describes the Massachusetts Bay Colony, and what would grow out of it, as a "city upon a hill." This becomes a defining image in American political speech for centuries.

**1689** John Locke's *Letter Concerning Toleration* is published. It helps convince American colonial thinkers that, in the words of George Mason, "all men should enjoy the fullest toleration in the exercise of religion."[1]

**July 4, 1776** The Continental Congress approves the final draft of the Declaration of Independence, which asserts that rights are endowed not by governments but by a Creator.

**September 17, 1786** The United States Constitution is adopted into law. Thomas Jefferson's Ordinance of Religious Freedom is adopted by the Virginia legislature. It assures that citizens will not be forced to support a church not of their choosing and that they will be free from harm in professing their religion.

**June 28, 1787** Benjamin Franklin moves that the delegates begin each day with prayer at the Constitutional Convention in Philadelphia. The convention does not act on his recommendation.

**July 13, 1787** Congress passes the Northwest Ordinance, which states that "religion, morality and knowledge being necessary also to good government and the happiness of mankind, schools and the means of education shall forever be encouraged."

**June 21, 1788** The United States Constitution is ratified by the states.

**December 15, 1791** Congress adopts the Bill of Rights, the first ten amendments to the US Constitution. The First Amendment reads, in part, "Congress shall make no law respecting the establishment of religion or prohibiting the free exercise thereof."

**September 19, 1796** George Washington issues his Farewell Address, in which he urges Americans to "with caution indulge the supposition that morality can be maintained without religion."[2]

**January 1, 1802** Thomas Jefferson writes a letter to the Danbury Baptist Association of Connecticut stating that his understanding of the First Amendment is that it builds "a wall of separation between Church and State."

**January 18, 1844** Senator James Buchanan, later US president, introduces a resolution in the Senate declaring the United States a Christian nation that acknowledges Jesus Christ as Savior. The resolution is rejected.

**April 22, 1864** The words "in God we trust" first appear on US coins.

**March 4, 1865** Abraham Lincoln gives his second inaugural address, in which he suggests that the Civil War was an act of divine judgment for the sin of slavery and calls the nation to "bind up" its wounds. The speech will be remembered as the greatest American political sermon.

**July 9, 1868** The Fourteenth Amendment to the Constitution is ratified. It provides, in part, that no state shall "deprive any person of life, liberty, or property without due process of law; nor deny to any person within its jurisdiction the equal protection of the laws."

**1875** The Blaine Amendment, which called for the incorporation of the Establishment Clause to the states, is defeated, as it would be twenty-five times between 1870 and 1950. This has been taken by some jurists and historians to mean that the adopters of the Fourteenth Amendment never intended to incorporate the Establishment Clause of the First Amendment to the States.

**July 10, 1925** The Scopes Monkey Trial begins in the Rhea County Court-house of Dayton, Tennessee. Eleven days later John Scopes is found guilty of teaching Darwinism. The media storm surrounding the trial portrays fundamentalist Christianity as silly and outdated.

**May 20, 1940** *Cantwell v. Connecticut.* The US Supreme Court holds for the first time that the Due Process Clause of the Fourteenth Amendment makes the Free Exercise Clause of the First Amendment applicable to the states.

**February 10, 1947** *Everson v. Board of Education.* The US Supreme Court makes Thomas Jefferson's phrase "wall of separation between Church and State" the meaning of the First Amendment's Establishment Clause and incorporates the clause to the states.

**July 2, 1954** Lyndon Johnson, then a senator from Texas, proposes an amendment to the IRS code that prevents 501(c)(3) organizations from influencing legislation or supporting candidates for public office under penalty of losing their tax-exempt status. The amendment passes without hearings or debate.

**September 12, 1960** Presidential candidate John Kennedy gives his famous speech on religion, defending his candidacy for president as a Roman Catholic, at the Rice Hotel in Houston.

**June 25, 1962** *Engel v. Vitale.* The US Supreme Court rules that a state-composed, nondenominational prayer violates the Establishment Clause of the First Amendment.

**February 8, 1964** Congress debates an amendment to the Civil Rights Act of 1963 that would remove protections for atheists. It passes in the House but is defeated in the Senate.

**June 1979** The Moral Majority is founded with Rev. Jerry Falwell as its spokesman.

**July 17, 1980** Ronald Reagan ends his nomination acceptance speech at the Republican National Convention by calling for "a moment of silent prayer."

**June 4, 1985** *Wallace v. Jaffree.* The US Supreme Court invalidates an Alabama law authorizing a one-minute period at the start of the school day "for meditation or voluntary prayer."

**November 16, 1993** Congress passes the Religious Freedom Restoration Act, which mandates that "government shall not substantially burden a person's exercise of religion even if the burden results from a rule of general applicability."

**June 19, 2000** *Santa Fe Independent School District v. Doe.* The US Supreme Court rules that student-led, student-initiated prayer at public school football games is a violation of the Establishment Clause of the First Amendment.

**June 28, 2006** Barack Obama gives his "Call to Renewal" speech at the Covenant for a New America Conference in Washington, DC.

**December 6, 2007** Mitt Romney gives his "Faith in America" speech, defending his candidacy for president as a Mormon, at the George Bush Presidential Library in College Station, Texas.

**January 21, 2010** *Citizens United v. Federal Election Commission.* The US Supreme Court holds that the First Amendment prohibits the government from restricting independent political expenditures by a non-profit corporation.

**March 2, 2011** *Snyder v. Phelps.* The US Supreme Court rules that a protest at the funeral of slain marine Matthew Snyder is protected by the First Amendment.

**June 26, 2015** *Obergefell v. Hodges.* The US Supreme Court rules that the Constitution guarantees same-sex couples a fundamental right to marry under both the Due Process Clause and the Equal Protection Clause of the Fourteenth Amendment.

# 6

# A Faith to Shape Her Politics

It is dangerous for a national candidate to say things that people might remember.

Eugene McCarthy

One of the wise women of our age was the poet and author Maya Angelou. She said a great deal that will be remembered, but one sentence in particular has proven surprisingly meaningful to the millions who have heard it. She said it while giving practical advice from her own experience. This bit of wisdom was, "When someone shows you who they are, believe them—the first time."

She intended these words as advice for dealing with difficult people, but they have become a guide for paying attention to people of every kind. It is wisdom that also applies, of course, to considering presidential candidates.

One of the ironies of our disregard for religion in American politics is that we often miss what people are trying to tell us about themselves. Even when candidates put their faith at the forefront of

151

their lives, we are likely not to see because something—our cynicism, our ignorance of religion, our certainty that faith is unrelated to politics—causes us to step around the subject, usually to focus on their less important traits.

Let us take, for example, the religious life of Hillary Clinton. She has tried to tell us who she is. She speaks of her faith often and insists it shapes her political views. Indeed, if the number of times she mentions faith publicly, the testimony of her staff, and her actions in office are any guide, Hillary Clinton is among the most religious politicians on the American scene today, as we shall see.

It's been hard to hear her. Part of the reason for this is that the faith emphasis of her opponents nearly always drowns her out. Republicans simply do religion better than Democrats. Their faith-based narratives nearly always overwhelm. Then Clinton's contest with Barack Obama for the Democratic presidential nomination in 2008 did not help. There was no competing with the noise of Jeremiah Wright or with Obama's seminal speeches about faith during that heated campaign. Senator Clinton's story of faith was barely heard.

There is another factor that is always at play in such things. In politics, we tend not to take seriously the faiths of those we oppose. We find it difficult to think someone wrong about governing but sincere in religion. They must be as false in spiritual matters as we think them wrongheaded in public policy. It is why a churchgoing, Bible-reading Barack Obama is accused of being a Muslim and a churchgoing, Bible-reading George W. Bush is accused of faking his faith for votes. Few politicians are able to convince more than half the country they might genuinely be devoted to God, so wide is the political divide in America today.

★   ★   ★

Hillary Clinton's story of faith is one we ought to know. She has been not only an outspoken first lady but also a senator from New

York and a secretary of state. She hopes one day to be president. Knowing who she is and what she believes have been and may continue to be important.

There is evidence she is sincere and that a lifelong religious vision shapes her thinking and defines her politics. There are the small things her staff reports. She carries a Bible in her purse, and she actually reads it. She speaks often of "grace notes," those daily, surprising connections between the human and the divine. It is common for her to begin a sentence at a staff meeting with the words, "The discipline of prayer dictates . . ." or "The method of Methodism teaches . . ."[1]

There are also the more public moments. Few will forget the time candidate Barack Obama spouted silliness about how embittered Americans "cling to guns and religion." It was another misstep by yet another Democratic candidate who spoke as though his party had no people of faith in it, as though all truly religious Americans were on the other side of the political aisle. Clinton could have remained silent to let Obama suffer from the damage he'd done. She didn't. She opened fire and defended those gun slingin' religious folks as sincere believers whose faith "is part of their whole being."[2]

She made missteps too, and some of them revealed her deepest spiritual longings. One came during some of the worst moments of her life. It was then that, however misguidedly, she sought refuge and comfort in an unusual form of the supernatural. It proved foolish and damaging, but it may have revealed a bit about the turn of her heart, as we will see.

★   ★   ★

To glimpse what meaning we can of Hillary Clinton's spiritual life, we should try to envision a scene from history. It is the mid-1700s and we are in the coalfields of northern England. Though it is midday, black is the color most visible. The sky is overcast, and beneath it and hovering low over the land are powdery billows of coal dust. It has taken captive everything in sight. The rude build-ings, the weary animals, the muddied ground are all smeared with it. The people reveal it most. Coal dust has invaded every part of them: their clothes, their faces, the whites of their eyes, the insides of their noses, and the folds of their skin. Over the years it has changed the color of Mother's hair. It is burned into the skin of Father's hands.

Their lives are grindingly hard. They are perfectly described in Thomas Hobbes's famous sentence: "No arts; no letters; no society; and which is worst of all, continual fear and danger of violent death; and the life of man, solitary, poor, nasty, brutish and short."[3]

There is only one figure wearing enough white to stand out from the general gloom. The coal-smeared workers have gathered to hear him speak. He is balancing on a box and is attired in a white wig, a white collar, and a black robe. The contrast of his clothes allows him to be seen at a distance, which helps today because nearly every miner and his family have gathered to hear what this stranger has to say.

His voice is high. Oddly, he is reading his sermon. It is odd because few of the miners can read. Most have never even seen a man read, much less heard one. In fact, many have never seen a preacher before.

In our modern imaginations, we would not tend to envision an eager response to this sermon. An Oxford don wearing a robe and reading his sermon to grubby, illiterate, coal-blackened workers is not a scene from which we would expect much.

Yet in the reality of the 1700s, much came. At the midpoint of the sermon, white streaks began to form on black-powdered faces. Sounds of weeping could soon be heard. They understood, these miners and their families. They caught what the preacher was trying to say. God loved them. Jesus died for them. Their day of salvation had come.

Laughing followed the weeping, much as it would throughout the months to come. Soon the whole nation would know. John Wesley had been at Kingswood. The Methodist revival had begun.

★　★　★

Something very much like this scene replayed often in the mind of Hillary Clinton when she was a child. It is among her earliest memories, for it was a tale told by her father, the most defining figure in her early years.

His name was Hugh Ellsworth Rodham. He was born in 1911 in Scranton, Pennsylvania. It was a mining town. Perhaps this is the reason the tale of Methodists preaching to coal miners in eighteenth-century England touched him so deeply.

He has often been compared to General George Patton. This was more for toughness than for fame or military bearing. The facts of his life tell the story. Determined to escape a miner's life, he fought hard to win a college football scholarship during his high school years. Penn State University offered. Hugh not only played on that storied football team but also graduated from the school with a degree. This was during the Great Depression.

He worked in the mines for a while after college before joining his father at the Scranton Lace Company. Soon after, he made his way to Chicago, where he sold curtains for a season. Then came news of bombs falling at a place called Pearl Harbor and the start of World War II. Hugh trained navy recruits and achieved the rank of chief petty officer. Afterward, he started a drapery and fabric business that he named Rodrik Fabrics. It was a brilliant decision. These were the postwar years. The GI Bill, suburban living, and a baby boom were remaking America. Home décor was all the rage. Hugh wisely located his business at the Merchandise Mart in Chicago's Loop, and he prospered.

He was a self-made man with a theology to match. God favored the self-reliant and the hardworking. Anything less displeased him. Hugh seldom went to church but loudly proclaimed a Methodist version of this God at home. His politics grew from this faith. He was a

Republican who opposed Franklin Roosevelt's New Deal and thought government handouts the sign of a weak and declining people.

He was hardworking, stubborn, successful, and almost entirely without ability to wrap his family in love. As Clinton biographer Gail Sheehy has written, "Pop-Pop, as the children called the authoritarian drillmaster at the head of the family, neither offered nor asked for nurturing. Matters of the heart were a fickle distraction in the Rodham household. Life was seen as combat."[4]

Hillary's mother was no pushover either. Dorothy Howell was born to teenaged parents in 1919. After they divorced, the eight-year-old was sent by train to live with a demanding grandmother in Los Angeles. By the time she turned fourteen, Dorothy could stand it no more. She left her grandmother's home and took a job as a nanny for a family who kindly taught her what family could mean. It changed her. She worked, she served, she studied, and she eventually finished high school. Soon after, her mother sent word that she had remarried and that her new husband would pay for Dorothy's college education.

It was a lie. When Dorothy returned to Chicago, she realized her mother merely needed a housekeeper. Wiser than her years, Dorothy escaped the trap set for her, found an apartment of her own, and began working menial jobs to get by. While applying for a job one day, she met a traveling salesman named Hugh Rodham. They married in 1942. Their first child, Hillary, was born in 1947.

Dorothy's imprint upon her daughter is captured in an incident that occurred when Hillary was only four years old. A neighborhood girl kept bullying her. In the manner of all four-year-olds, she ran home to her mother in tears. Dorothy was not like other mothers, though. Instead of the protective hugs that Hillary probably expected, she heard these words: "There's no room in this house for cowards! The next time she hits you, I want you to hit her back!" Hillary did. The bullying stopped. The boys looking on viewed Hillary with new respect. She ran home and told Dorothy, "I can play with the boys now!"[5] Both mother and child remembered this as a turning point. Dorothy's steel and Hugh's self-reliance fashioned much of the woman Hillary became.

The unusual journeys of Hillary's parents aside, the Rodham home was fairly typical of Middle America at the time. "We talked with God," Hillary remembered later. "We walked with God, ate, studied, and argued with God. Each night we knelt by our beds to pray."[6]

It was Methodism raw and compassionate that set her on her life's path. At her family's Park Ridge Methodist Church, she heard the famous words of John Wesley: "Do all the good you can, by all the means you can, in all the ways you can, at all the times you can, to all the people you can, as long as you ever can."[7] They captured her, bright and eager to do good in the world as she was. Visions of Methodists preaching at English coal mines filled her imagination. They formed, for her, a summons to make a difference.

Her mentor in this vision of Christianity was Don Jones, a recent Drew University seminary graduate who entered her life when she was just thirteen. As the new youth minister at her church, Jones arrived ready to break from the sleepy ways of youth ministers past, eager to thrust his charges into confrontation with the crises of the age. He was just "cool" enough to do it. He arrived at Park Ridge driving a red sports car, his blond hair blowing free in the wind. His self-confidence arrived with him. He was certain of all he had learned in the classrooms of Drew.

It was 1961. John F. Kennedy was president. The biggest news story of the year was a crisis caused by Russian missiles in Cuba. The Supreme Court had already determined to hear a case that would move it to ban prayer in public schools the next year. Change loomed for America. Yet the innocence of the 1950s lingered. Elvis was still in the army. The Beatles had yet to arrive. Folk music and Beat poetry filled the air. In 1960, *Ben Hur* had been movie of the year. In 1961, it was *West Side Story*.

To his credit, Jones was in tune with the simmering unrest in the country. He wanted those under his ministry to be relevant to it all. He had determined that his youth program would be built upon Jesus and John Wesley but also the voices of dissent that were just then beginning to lash the nation's soul. There was a revolution coming. He didn't think Jesus would want his students to miss it.

The teenagers of Park Ridge Methodist never forgot Jones or his methods. He called his Thursday night meetings "the University of Life." Previous youth ministers had taught from stale denominational curricula and worried that the young weren't engaged. Jones used experiences to inspire and transform. One night he asked the group to meditate while Bob Dylan's "A Hard Rain's A-Gonna Fall" sounded in their ears. On other evenings he read poetry to them, asked them to help D. H. Lawrence refute Plato, and used a rented movie projector to show art house films—Francois Truffaut's *400 Blows* and Rod Serling's *Requiem for a Heavyweight* among them.

He was fearless. He invited an atheist to debate the existence of God as his wide-eyed youth looked on and led a discussion of teen pregnancy that set the whole congregation abuzz.

He regularly loaded his teens into a bus and took them to parts of town they would not have otherwise seen. He once merged his privileged white youth with a church group from the inner city and gathered them all around a print of Picasso's *Guernica*, a painting of the devastations of war. Discussion followed, with Hillary's friends speaking of war only in the most abstract terms. Then, after a silence, one inner-city girl quietly said, "Just last week, my uncle drove up and parked on the street and some guy came up to him and said you can't park there, that's my parking place, and my uncle resisted him and the guy pulled out a gun and shot him."[8] The more privileged white youth were stunned, Hillary in particular, and this experience evolved into one of the most important experiences of their lives: a trip to hear Martin Luther King Jr. speak at Chicago's Orchestra Hall in April 1962.

Jones did not fail to notice his impact on Hillary. Recognizing her intelligence and drive, he urged her to read the authors who had won him in school: Tillich, Niebuhr, Kierkegaard, and Bonhoeffer. He met with her regularly to hear her thoughts. He did not hesitate to suggest both J. D. Salinger's *Catcher in the Rye* and a Methodist devotional, Beat author Jack Kerouac and the Bible. He wanted this gifted girl to be captured by the single idea that had most captured him: Christianity is a faith that either relieves the suffering of others or is dead.

She became his willing convert. She read voraciously and threw herself into food drives, ministry to migrant workers, and protests as Jones encouraged. She was impressionable. When Jones introduced her to the thought of leading radical Saul Alinksy, the profane agnostic author of *Reveille for Radicals*, Hillary was cautious at first but became so impressed by him that she later wrote her college thesis on the man.

Jones and his methods were controversial. Families left Park Ridge because of him. Complaints were written. Committees met. Explanations and defenses were given. Eventually, he would have to leave. When the time came, he had already imparted enough of his version of Christianity to set Hillary Rodham on fire.

She would carry Jones's version of the Methodist social gospel to Wellesley, to Yale Law School, and into marriage to the Baptist Bill Clinton. During these years, her devotion to social causes vastly outweighed her interest in the core of the Christian gospel: the person of Jesus, the work of the Spirit, prayer, worship, the scriptures, and changing the world with God's power. Instead, she had begun discovering her gifts, feeling the power of her intellect and her verbal command. She also found that she enjoyed troubling authority. She admitted she once took a black friend to her all-white church just to stir things up. She often spoke up in class, but even her friends said, "It sometimes had an edge to it."[9]

One story in particular reveals her manner at this time. As president of her class at Wellesley, she was invited to be one of the speakers at her own graduation ceremony. She worked hard on every detail of her speech. When the moment finally arrived, she was prepared. Yet at the last minute, she decided to discard the notes in her hand and instead give a point-by-point refutation of the commencement speech delivered moments before by a black Republican US senator named Edward W. Brooke. For nearly ten minutes she was fierce and unrestrained. When she finished, the students gave her a standing ovation. Their parents were appalled. An excerpt of her talk appeared in *Life* magazine and in a front-page article of the *Boston Globe*.

After her graduation from Yale Law School in 1973, she served as an attorney for the Children's Defense Fund in Cambridge and then for the congressional committee working to impeach Richard Nixon. She had grown increasingly radical in her politics. Even her husband was sometimes surprised. She could be found wherever the hard edge of the political left was on nearly any issue, but she was seldom found in church and seldom found with an open Bible. Some friends who knew her well at this time saw little hint of a meaningful faith.

There followed the Clintons' storied rise through Arkansas politics to the White House in 1992. During these years, Hillary was plagued by a crisis of perception that she "had no religion" and that she was, in truth, "a godless liberal."[10] She found these allegations painful. She thought of herself as a woman of prayer and Bible study who could quote Wesley at length and speak warmly and comfortably of

160

God's work in her life. Her critics pointed to her absence from church, her far left politics, and her grinding ambition as evidence that any religion she had was a façade, that she faked faith for political gain.

She took steps to change her public image in matters of faith. While her husband was governor of Arkansas, she realized that in the culture around her, religion was too tightly packaged with politics to ignore. She began attending Little Rock's First United Methodist Church while Bill attended Immanuel Baptist, pastored by the revered W. O. Vaught. She also began teaching Sunday school and acquired a reputation for a talk entitled "Why I Am a United Methodist." A selection from a similar speech of this time reveals her vision of Methodism.

> As a member of the British Parliament, [Wesley] spoke out for the poor at a time when their lives were being transformed by far-reaching industrial and economic changes. He spent the rest of his life evangelizing among the same people he had spoken up for in Parliament. He preached a gospel of social justice demanding as determinedly as ever that society do right by all its people. But he also preached a gospel of personal responsibility, asking every man and woman to take responsibility for their own lives . . . and cultivate the habits that would make them productive.[11]

It is intriguing that little in this portion of Clinton's speech is historically true. Wesley never served in Parliament, and he would not have recognized his gospel in her description. The speech reveals more about her than it does Wesley, and this was part of her problem during the Little Rock years.

Still, there were genuine signs of renewed faith during this time. She traveled with her husband on a trip to Israel led by W. O. Vaught. Both of the Clintons have referred to this as transitional in their lives. In her "Why I Am a United Methodist" talk, she did sometimes speak of her personal relationship with God and of spiritual experiences that had begun to define her in her youth. This emphasis became more pronounced each time she spoke. Her pastor at the time recalled, "One of her favorite thoughts was that the goal of life is to restore what has been lost, to find oneness with God, and until we find this we are lonely."[12]

If she had indeed experienced a deeper connection to God and found the answer to her loneliness, it came at the right moment. She would need it all when she learned of her husband's infidelities. This was a torturous time that could have ended with the death of the marriage. Instead, the Clintons sought help, including the help of Hillary's Methodist pastor. In time, they reported they had forgiven, healed, and renewed their vows. This reconciliation is often reported as, at least in part, fruit of a renewed Christian faith in Hillary's life.

Yet she was no less suspect in matters of religion by the time the Clintons entered the White House in 1993. The criticism and the accusations threatened to overwhelm. She seemed constantly forced to do damage control.

★　★　★

In 1994, for example, Hillary agreed to do an interview with Kenneth Woodward of *Newsweek*. It was an opportunity to fully explain the religious life she cited so often and to a reporter she deemed safe. Woodward already accepted as fact that the Clintons were perhaps the most openly religious first couple that century had seen. Still, he pressed Hillary about her claim that she was an "old-fashioned Methodist," and this led to a grilling of the kind usually reserved for new converts.

Woodward: "Do you believe in the Father, Son, and Holy Spirit?"
First Lady: "Yes."
Woodward: "The atoning death of Jesus?"

162

First Lady: "Yes."

Woodward: "The resurrection of Christ?"

First Lady: "Yes."[13]

It was after this interrogation that she made her mistake. This was part of the problem. There was always a mistake to be fixed. This time it happened because she overreached. Woodward's questions had likely knocked her off balance. She reported that she kept a copy of *The Book of Resolutions of the United Methodist Church* along with her Bible at her bedside. This was hard to believe. The snickering was nearly audible throughout Washington, DC.

It grew only louder when she added, "I think that the Methodist Church, for a period of time, became too socially concerned, too involved in the social gospel, and did not pay enough attention to questions of personal salvation and individual faith."[14] This did not sound like the Hillary Clinton Americans knew. It did not sound like Don Jones's disciple, nor did it sound like the Hillary Clinton of the "Why I Am a United Methodist" speech. Members of the media had long before become convinced that if Hillary Clinton was a "social gospel Methodist," hers was a faith more social than gospel. Certainly, no one thought she leaned more to Jesus and salvation than she did to causes and protests.

In the interview with Woodward, she tried to urge otherwise. She spoke of reading Christian authors like Henri Nouwen, Gordon MacDonald, and Tony Campolo. Critics guffawed and heard nothing in this but a skilled politician making the required religious claims. The interview rang false and fueled conservative talk radio for months.

★  ★  ★

There is some tragedy in this. If Hillary was indeed reading these particular authors at this time, it may have been because she was genuinely yearning for a deeper connection to God. The truth is she may have been in desperate need of help.

She had endured one of the most soul-crushing experiences a woman can know: her husband's unfaithfulness. Bill Clinton was infamous as a man of unchecked appetites who bedded women with frequency—Hillary's friends among them—and enlisted staff in the cover-ups. His behavior was devastating to her. Always there were the tearful confessions. Always there were the promises and the pleas. Divorce loomed, but each time it did, a counselor urged healing. Some force—was it ambition? Faith? Love? Their daughter?—kept Bill and Hillary together.

Then the name Monica Lewinsky moved to the center of the national stage. Semen-stained dresses and cigars used for intercourse and discussions of whether oral sex is actually sex filled headlines. An investigator named Kenneth Starr made sure the nation knew it all. Once again Hillary Clinton had to contend with what her husband visited upon her. This time it all occurred in the White House. This time the whole world was watching.

She endured. She always did. Whatever it was—an unfaithful husband, the Republican barrage, the pain that befalls a woman of strength. She was wounded, though, and in need of something more than she'd known. This is what made her do it. She and her husband had welcomed a wide variety of religious leaders to the White House. Some were of the New Age type, and it was one of these, Jean Houston, who made the suggestion that caused so much trouble.

Hillary had always identified with Eleanor Roosevelt and sometimes even mentioned imaginary conversations with her hero in speeches. It was a mistake, but it gave Houston enough to work with. According to Bob Woodward's account in *The Choice*, Houston urged Hillary to "search further and deeper" into her devotion to Eleanor. The first lady apparently agreed. Soon after, Houston arranged a meeting in the White House solarium. It is possible that Hillary had no idea what Houston intended, but in the retelling, this meeting appeared to be little more than a séance. According to Woodward:

> Hillary addressed Eleanor, focusing on her predecessor's fierceness and determination, her advocacy on behalf of people in need. Hillary continued to address Eleanor, discussing the obstacles, the criticism, the loneliness the former First Lady felt. Her identification with Mrs. Roosevelt was intense and personal. They were members of an exclusive club of women who could comprehend the complexity, the ambiguity of their position. It's hard, Hillary said. Why was there such a need in people to put other people down? . . . I was misunderstood, Hillary replied, her eyes still shut, speaking as Mrs. Roosevelt. You have to do what you think is right, she continued. It was crucial to set a course and hold it.[15]

This went on for some time. With the doors to the spirit world opened, Houston also tried making contact with Mahatma Gandhi and even Jesus Christ, according to Woodward. Something about this didn't seem right, and it was then that Hillary brought the session to an end.

This meeting was so clumsy, so ill-advised, that it is a wonder a woman of Hillary Clinton's political sense would allow it to occur. Among the few understandable reasons for it is that she was at the end of herself, that her loneliness, hurt, and confusion drove her to it.

It was not the kind of thing that would remain a secret. Of course it got out. Of course she was once again betrayed. She should have known. In fact, she likely did. She was desperate, though, and willing to risk.

The news confirmed her critics' suspicions that she was self-absorbed to the point of imbalance and far from the Christian she claimed to be. Even her supporters were concerned that the first lady would allow such weirdness to take place in the White House. How could the smart and sophisticated Hillary Clinton allow herself to come under the influence of a carnival palm reader like Jean Houston?

Hillary did her best to give assurances: "The bottom line is, I have no spiritual advisors or any other alternatives to my deeply held Methodist faith and traditions on which I have relied since childhood."[16] She even tried humor. At the start of a speech one evening she said, "I have just had an imaginary talk with First Lady Roosevelt, and she thinks this is a terrific idea."[17]

She could not pierce the animosity, though. She could not win back what was lost. Words like *sleaze*, *evil*, and *demonic* were blended with *controlling*, *liberal*, and *unhinged* to form an unwanted epitaph over her White House years. Don Jones, then a professor of social ethics at Drew University, still advised her but could not rescue her, nor would her unending attempts to fashion something new and noble. When she spoke of a "politics of meaning" and of using "God-given gifts" to heal society, it fell flat. If she spoke of connecting the spiritual to the political or blending the best of conservative and liberal policies, it sounded to both sides of the aisle like so much pious mush. She seemed unable to craft a legacy equal to her spiritual vision.

When the Clinton presidency ended in 2001, many Americans thought of Bill and Hillary in the terms used by conservative speechwriter Peggy Noonan for her *Wall Street Journal* column. After the Clintons' departure, Noonan said, the White House would need an exorcism.

> I think that all places of concentrated power have within them the devil's little imps—little imps, unseen, sitting on the cornice of the doorway in this office, giggling quietly in a corner on a bookcase in that one. . . . All White Houses have them. But in the one just ending

the imps ran wild. It would be a very good and important thing if Mr. Bush invited in a fine and good priest, a wise and deep rabbi, a faithful and loving minister, and had them pray together in that house, and reanoint it, and send the imps, at least for a while, on their way.[18]

It was a view shared by many Americans. Something dark and damaging was coming to an end. But this was Hillary Rodham Clinton they were talking about, and she knew it. She had only wanted to do good, she said. She had only wanted to end suffering as God ordained. Now people actually thought she had left demons in the president's house, the spiritual droppings of a demonic reign.

She was not done. This could not be the final word. She could not let the White House years be the end. Soon she decided to run for the Senate from New York. The Clintons purchased a home in Chappaqua, New York, and Hillary launched into a bruising campaign in which she and her opponent spent over $90 million. She won in a blowout, with 55 percent of the vote to her opponent's 43 percent. It was an historic victory. For the first time, a former first lady was elected to the United States Senate.

This came in 2000, just as George W. Bush was entering office following one of the most faith-based campaign feuds in American history. Then came the horrors of September 11, 2001.

American culture began to change in many ways that day, and among them was a renewed emphasis on faith. There was a greater openness about God and about spiritual things and what they meant for the nation. The freshman senator from New York seemed to drink in this new spirit and make it her own. Perhaps there had been a restoration during her White House years, born of the humiliation and the pain. Perhaps it had even begun long before in Little Rock when she had been forced to play the southern governor's wife—with the teas and the churchgoing and the prayers. Maybe she hadn't felt it then, but perhaps over time it had become real and helped to restore what Wellesley, Yale, and life with Bill had taken from her soul. Some suspected it was all strategic posturing by a discerning politician who understood the religious trends of her times.

Whatever the cause, there was a visible change. She spoke of God often, seemed at ease with her faith, and took steps that astonished friends and political enemies alike. She regularly attended Capitol Hill prayer meetings and even appeared at a faith-based event sponsored by Republican majority leader Tom DeLay, one of the men who had worked tirelessly to impeach her husband. She frequented conferences like those sponsored by Sojourners, the progressive Christian organization that stressed the priority of social justice in the service of God. When she did, she often spoke casually about the writings of Thomas Aquinas or St. Augustine. It ceased to feel forced when she talked about sensing "the presence of the Holy Spirit on many occasions" or filled her speeches with scripture and references to prayer.[19]

Yet Hillary Clinton's Senate years betray the tension between faith and policy that would follow her through her 2008 presidential campaign and to the end of her time as secretary of state. As open as she had become about religion, it was sometimes hard for even members of her own party to find a direct and understandable connection between her faith and her politics.

In her early Senate career, she appeared to be a moderate. Some said she was merely being pragmatic, as might be expected of a politician contemplating a run for the White House. She supported President George W. Bush's decision to invade Iraq, for example. She also took stands on moral issues like teen abstinence and the immorality of Hollywood films. Because of these and other views, she was accused of betraying the political left for the safe ground of the comfortable middle. The Associated Press described her as "a Northeastern centrist."[20] The *New York Times* expressed its disappointment by claiming that Clinton "has defied simple ideological labeling since joining the Senate, ending up in the political center on issues like health care, welfare, abortion, morality and values and national defense, to name a few."[21]

The ratings of leading political watchdog organizations tell a different tale. Liberal groups normally gave her high ratings. Americans for Democratic Action, for example, rated her at 95 percent. The AFL-CIO gave her 93 percent. As expected, conservative groups gave her low ratings. The American Conservative Union gave her a meager 11 percent, while the National Taxpayers Union rated her only 14 percent.

On religious and social issues, the pattern was the same. The Christian Coalition and the National Right to Life Committee both put her at zero. Meanwhile, the National Abortion and Reproductive Rights Action League gave her a stunning 100 percent.[22]

In his valuable book *God and Hillary Clinton*, political historian Paul Kengor summarized the conclusions of the nonpartisan *National Journal*: In 2002, "not a single U.S. senator was more liberal on economic and social matters than Mrs. Clinton, and in 2003, no senator surpassed her liberal ranking on social issues."[23]

During these years, she was on the left edge of the Senate, to the left even of her own left-leaning United Methodist denomination. Her positions on abortion and same-sex marriage alone tell the tale. She voted against a ban on partial-birth abortion, a procedure in which a child is partially delivered from the womb in order to suction out the brain before full delivery. Some members of her own party called this "infanticide." She worked to block the appointments of two pro-life conservatives to the Supreme Court, insisting that she did not trust the two eminent jurists to protect "fundamental rights." By this she meant unrestricted abortion.

She abandoned her original views on traditional marriage as defined in the Defense of Marriage Act (DOMA)—which her husband had signed and she had defended with biblical references—and she became an outspoken champion of same-sex marriage. She cited as a reason "the guiding principles of my faith."[24] Years later, when the US Supreme Court issued its landmark ruling on same-sex marriage in 2015, she was among the most visible to celebrate.

Yet she held these and other positions while also attempting to hold the high ground of religious principle. In 2006, Republicans supported an immigration bill she opposed. "It is certainly not in keeping with my understanding of the scriptures," she scolded. "This bill would liberally criminalize the Good Samaritan—and probably even Jesus himself."[25] She expressed her disappointment with John Kerry's loss to George W. Bush in 2004 by insisting, "No one can read the New Testament of our Bible without recognizing that Jesus had a lot more to say about how we treat the poor than most of the issues that were talked about in this election."[26]

She also learned to invoke her spirituality while remaining stunningly vague about the issues at hand. In defining her politics, she once said, "The very core of what I believe is this concept of individual worth, which I think flows from all of us being creatures of God and being imbued with a spirit."[27] This was sentiment without meaning, spirituality without substance. It invoked much but specified little.

It was sometimes difficult to know if faith drew any firm lines in her thinking. She had long argued that people of faith should be permitted to "live out their faith in the public square." Yet in 2015, during a Women in the World Summit in New York, Clinton spoke of the priority of abortion rights and insisted that to protect these rights "deep-seated cultural codes, religious beliefs and structural biases have to be changed."[28] This led many to wonder if she welcomed people of faith to the public square but allowed them to stay only if they were willing to change their faith when her politics required.

Questions like this arose again in July 2015 when videos began surfacing that seemed to depict Planned Parenthood officials negotiating the sale of organs harvested from aborted fetuses. One of the videos captured a Planned Parenthood medical director describing—over wine and appetizers at a favorite restaurant—how a fetus can be "crushed" so as to preserve livers, lungs, and "intact" hearts. A second video released days later appeared to depict a Planned Parenthood official negotiating prices for fetal tissue and joking, "I want a Lamborghini." This official also described the "crunchy" procedures used to harvest fetal organs.

When Clinton spoke publicly about these videos, some Americans hoped they might hear wisdom from her faith, perhaps the balanced approach possible for a woman who valued human life, as she often said, because it was made in the image of God. Instead, Clinton expressed no outrage over the possibility that Planned Parenthood had illegally harvested and sold fetal organs for profit or grief over the suffering of the child taken from the womb. Her outrage was reserved for the critics of Planned Parenthood. She even described the typical woman seeking an abortion as doing so "based on her faith."[29]

★   ★   ★

It rankles Clinton's critics to speak of her as "faith-based." Yet the fact is that she is among the most religion-oriented politicians of our time, as we have seen. She has openly admitted that her religious views shaped her thinking—and thus often her vote—on immigration, on abortion, on gay rights, on the definition of marriage, on welfare, and on a wide variety of women's issues.

Though she is one of the most visible women in the world, though her every public word is recorded and archived, and though she speaks often of her religion, it is difficult to pin down the meaning of her faith for her politics. We cannot refer to a Methodist handbook.

She has moved far beyond even those broad confines. We cannot refer to the counsel of Don Jones. He passed away in 2009. There is no systematic statement of what Clinton believes. We gain what insight we can through a few words in official statements, from casual comments of meaning, and sometimes even from the events she chooses to attend.

Yet Hillary Clinton hopes to lead the most powerful nation in the world. If she does, she will take her unique brand of faith with her. It will guide her in the Oval Office should she be successful. It will counsel her as she ponders options. It will sustain her as she endures the bludgeoning that is modern political leadership. It will frame all that she does both in word and in deed. She has said as much herself.

Support her or oppose her, we are obligated to know her religion as well as we can. Her faith, as with a majority of American politicians, is at the heart of her politics. We will have to ask the relevant questions and ask them often. She is religiously a work in progress, often reforming and remaking what she believes. This means voters must be vigilant. We need to know more than we have been allowed to know before of how Hillary Clinton, and every person who leads us, is shaped by their religion.

# 7

# The Narrative of Faith

I believe today that my conduct is in accordance with the will of the Almighty Creator.

Adolf Hitler

We get our news today in bits and pieces. We catch a title one minute, an unrelated statistic an hour later. Perhaps an anecdote or two stick in our minds. We remember news photos we've seen but not the stories that go with them. We remember feeling an emotion about something we read but can't recall the details. It makes us feel as fragmented at times as our understanding of the news is almost all the time.

This doesn't matter much when it comes to sports news and weather reports. We miss a game. We end up getting caught in the rain. It's not a big deal. However, if we constantly miss the truth about people running for office, we distance ourselves from the vital world of politics and government and may also vote stupidly—or, if we don't think we know enough to even mark a ballot, not vote at all. Both are tragic, for us and for the nation.

Fortunately, absorbing what is important about the faith of political candidates is on the easier end of all we need to know. Here's the secret: information about faith should form itself into a story, into a narrative we can tell over a meal or a visit with friends. This also helps us determine if we know enough about a candidate's religious beliefs and practices. Can we tell the story of a candidate's faith? Have we learned enough for the narrative arc to form? Has it congealed in our minds so we can see the whole, so that it has a meaningful beginning, middle, and end?

Faith isn't economics. It isn't learned by memorizing unfamiliar terms and swirling numbers. It isn't that disconnected. A person's faith is always a story. It might come with new language. It might require grasping a few unfamiliar concepts. Still, it is usually just the tale of a heart's journey through time. Embed that tale in politics and there may be less heart and more journey, but it should all still weave itself into a fascinating tale.

This is the question to ask ourselves, then, before we start asking questions of our candidates: What is this person's story of faith, and what will it likely mean when he or she gets into office?

## The Journey to Faith

We begin to understand a person's faith only when we understand his or her journey to it. How a person comes to faith is often as revealing as what that individual believes afterward. For some, there is an instantaneous and dramatic conversion from old to new. For others, faith arrives slowly, in such an unhurried progression that there is no transitional day or moment. There are only transitional years. Most people in the world absorb their faith with their mother's milk. They are born into a religion, a family, and a way of life all at once. They will have to make this religion their own over time, but their journey is always as part of a community, their religion with them from the beginning.

These tales of the journey to faith imprint believers' lives all their days. The more the story is told, the greater its meaning and the more defining it becomes. For sincere people of faith, little is as revealing of who they are as the story they have to tell about coming to faith. Consider Barack Obama's now well-known description of his conversion.

> It was because of these newfound understandings—that religious commitment did not require me to suspend critical thinking, disengage from the battle for economic and social justice, or otherwise retreat from the world that I knew and loved—that I was finally able to walk down the aisle of Trinity United Church of Christ one day and be baptized. It came about as a choice and not an epiphany; the questions I had did not magically disappear. But kneeling beneath that cross on the South Side of Chicago, I felt God's spirit beckoning me. I submitted myself to His will, and dedicated myself to discovering His truth.[1]

There are hardly better words to capture what we can know of the man and his brand of faith. There are the traditions: the God of scripture, a church, and a cross. There is also the Obama we have come to know. He is a man who sees the world in shades of gray rather than in black and white. He is always thinking, ever pondering variations on a theme, constantly holding himself in reserve until the verdict is in. He never ceases to be the scholar, the jurist, and the academician. Even at conversion. Always there are questions. Always there are conditions. He might devote himself to God but only after he is sure his prior commitments are safe: critical thinking, social justice, and the world.

He presents himself as the even-tempered man of reason coming to faith. No magic happened, he tells us. There was no epiphany. In his "Call to Renewal" speech, he even says of this moment, "I didn't fall out." He doesn't want us to confuse him with the overwrought or the overheated. He cannot be overcome. He wants us to know he made a rational decision. What we see here is the enduring nature of the man. It helps us to know him—personally and politically. In fact, it helps us to know him in all of his life and thus to better understand his imprint on our age.

To approach a conversion story so as to better understand the convert is no insult to the spiritual themes in the tale. Conversion stories are by definition a meeting of the human and the divine. They are revealing of both. We should not be put off by what they expose of the one converted. The characteristics we glimpse in what is usually a raw and unguarded moment help us understand the soul that will emerge afterward. When politicians tell their conversion stories, it usually means they are offering it as a window into knowing who they are. We should pay attention.

These stories of the journey to faith can be so revealing that some public figures rework them in the retelling to control their meaning. Usually this is an attempt at privacy. Sometimes it is an attempt at editing for popular appeal. Occasionally, it is a cynical effort to add meaning to the experience that was not there originally.

George W. Bush reworked his conversion story when he told it. This doesn't mean he was insincere, but it does mean he was trying to shape the story so as to manage its meaning. In his autobiography, *A Charge to Keep: My Journey to the White House,* he recalls the time in 1985 when his family met with Billy Graham at the Bush home in Kennebunkport, Maine. On one memorable, fire-lit evening, Graham sat with the family and informally answered their questions. "I don't remember the exact words," George W. later recalled. "It was more the power of his example. The Lord was so clearly reflected in his gentle and loving demeanor." Sometime afterward, Bush and Graham went for a stroll on Walker's Point. As they walked the beach, Graham asked Bush, "Are you right with God?" "No," Bush replied, "but I want to be."

Bush was moved by how it felt to be in Graham's presence: "I knew I was in the presence of a great man. He was like a magnet; I felt drawn to seek something different. He didn't lecture or admonish; he shared warmth and concern. Billy Graham didn't make you feel guilty; he made you feel loved."[2] Then came the change: "Reverend Graham planted a mustard seed in my soul, a seed that grew over the next year. I had always been a religious person, had regularly attended church, even taught Sunday school and served as an altar boy. But that weekend my faith took on new meaning. It was the beginning of a new walk where I would recommit my heart to Jesus Christ. I was humbled to learn that God sent His Son to die for a sinner like me."[3]

It was all true, but it was not all the truth. There were other stages in the tale, other steps toward faith that Bush chose not to tell. Years before, in a time of spiritual desperation, he had asked for a private appointment with an evangelist who was holding mass meetings in Midland/Odessa. The evangelist's name was Arthur Blessitt. He was a fiery preacher with the common touch who had become famous for carrying a twelve-foot cross around the world and meeting with global leaders like Pope John Paul II and Yasser Arafat.

When friends arranged time with Blessitt, Bush told the evangelist, "Arthur, I did not feel comfortable attending the meeting, but I want to talk to you about how to know Jesus Christ and how to follow Him."[4]

Blessitt pondered this and then asked, "What is your relationship with Jesus?"

"I'm not sure," Bush replied.

"Let me ask you this question," Blessitt probed. "If you died this moment, do you have the assurance you would go to heaven?"

"No," Bush replied.

Blessitt appreciated the honesty. The young man before him was famous as the son of the nation's vice president. He was also known for his failures and defeats. Blessitt could see the lingering pain in Bush's face. The evangelist spoke for a few moments about what it meant to be a Christian, and then he led Bush in prayer. He ended with the words, "I accept the Lord Jesus Christ as my Savior and desire to be a true believer in and follower of Jesus. Thank you, God, for hearing my prayer. In Jesus' name I pray."[5]

That Bush recounted the weekend with Graham in his autobiography and not the earlier encounter with Blessitt is revealing. Perhaps Bush viewed the earlier meeting as only one in a series of steps that carried him to a final conversion with Graham. Perhaps he thought the Graham story would be easier for his readers to digest. He may have preferred the memory of a gentle conversion on a New England beach at the hands of the most respected evangelist in the world to the memory of a desperate failure meeting secretly with a street preacher because he was too embarrassed to be seen with the man in public.

Whatever the case, Bush's journey to faith is as revealing as Obama's. We know Bush as two men: the Harvard- and Yale-educated son of a famous family, born to privilege and wealth, and the crude son of west Texas, born to a plainspoken mother and a father of daunting success. His journey to faith reveals both the hard-edged and the elegant in his life, the New England and the west Texas in his soul. This is the nature of George W. Bush, and his conversion story speaks of it all. We cannot know him unless we understand this story and reflect even on the way he chooses to tell it.

Occasionally, politicians recount their conversions so as to obscure, and this, too, has meaning. When Sarah Palin wrote *Going Rogue* after her tumultuous experience as John McCain's vice presidential running mate, she recounted her journey to faith in very guarded terms. After quoting Blaise Pascal, she told of an experience at an Assembly of God summer camp in Alaska during the 1970s.

Looking around at the incredible creation that is Alaska—the majestic peaks and midnight sun, the wild waters and teeming wildlife—I could practically see and hear and feel God's spirit reflected in everything in nature. I reasoned that if God knew what He was doing in this magnificent creation, how much more did He know about me? If He is powerful and wise enough to make all this and though also to create a speck like me, there surely must be a plan, and He'd know more than I did about my future and my purpose. I made the conscious decision that summer to put my life in my Creator's hands and trust Him as I sought my life's path.[6]

This was Palin expressing her story through the poetry of nature, but it was also Palin, bloodied and bruised from her vice presidential campaign, unwilling to put another weapon in her critics' hands. She was a daughter of Pentecostalism. How could the American media begin to understand? She worshiped with people who raised their hands, spoke in tongues, cast out demons, and prayed for healing. She couldn't possibly put her faith fully on the page.

She was weary of YouTube videos of her church's services being replayed for laughs, and she was angry that people she loved had to endure verbal beatings nationwide for what they believed. In *Going Rogue*, then, she spoke of her faith honestly, but she disguised it, using terms any environmentalist or her nemesis Barack Obama might understand. It wasn't all the truth, but it was some of the truth, and it was certainly as much as she was willing to say.

As with Obama and Bush, the way the story was told is revealing. Palin was an accomplished woman asked to step up to a broader national stage. When she did, she was celebrated but also pilloried for being a rube. She wasn't that different from most Americans. She had her gifts, had known her success but hungered for more. She was both ambitious and genuinely eager to serve. She was punished for it, though, because the guardians of power thought her out of her depth. Her faith became a punch line. So did her family. This made her angry. She couldn't prevent it on the campaign trail, but afterward she refused to arm her enemies. So she wrote her faith story in the broadest possible terms and kept its details to herself and those she trusted. Both her guardedness and her anger endure, evident in nearly every public word she speaks.

The stories of Obama, Bush, and Palin coming to faith are not unlike the stories of other believers. They are pregnant with meaning. They betray truth in the facts that are told and the facts concealed, in the weave of the journey and the conclusions made. When they are done, we know much more than we did before. It is knowledge that is vital to understanding who each of them is and what their leadership means to the country.

## Heritage

A faith is not just a gaggle of individual beliefs. It is a lens through which we view reality. Part of what we see when we look through that lens is the past, a history that our faith helps to narrate. This has vast power to define us because human beings have an innate need to feel themselves part of a story—a purpose—that flows out of the past and moves through them into the future. Their faith shapes the lessons the past has to teach and what it will mean for them in the future.

As we have seen, Hillary Clinton's sense of heritage was powerfully defined by her family's Methodist memories.

> Historically my father's family was always Methodist and took it very seriously. Mine is a family who traces our roots back to Bristol, England, to the coal mines and the Wesleys. So as a young child I would hear stories that my grandfather had heard from his parents,

180

who heard them from their parents who were all involved in the great evangelical movement that swept England.[7]

She absorbed these memories and took possession of them as a model for her life. She also redefined them and lived them out in ways undreamt of by her parents or by her Methodist forbearers. These memories, these emblems of heritage, are an essential part of her understanding of who she is in the world. Her sense of purpose is shaped by the sense that she descends from a crusading, reforming, even combative global movement. We cannot know her or her politics apart from knowing that she believes this about herself.

George W. Bush also sees himself in terms of heritage. He is descended from a long line of adventurers, preachers, war heroes, and politicians. The greatest man he has ever known is his father. This is all part of his heritage by birth, and it comes with a spiritual and emotional inheritance that never ceases to work in him.

When he became an evangelical in the mid-1980s, his mentors urged him to familiarize himself with the Christian vision of the American founding fathers. He did, and it profoundly affected him. It gave him a sense of purpose that is behind the titles of his two autobiographies. He believes he has a *Charge to Keep*, both from God and from earlier generations. This is both a duty of service to fulfill and a commission to preserve what has been entrusted to him. It calls for *Decision Points*, the title of his presidential autobiography. As he understands it, he keeps the charge of God, the founding fathers, and his own ancestors by making decisions, usually in times of crisis and often against fierce opposition. This is the price of standing for heritage in a rootless, unaware, troubled generation.

Bush put his belief into poetic expression when he spoke at the 9/11 commemoration service at the National Cathedral shortly after that day of crashing planes and crumbling buildings. In perhaps the best line in one of the best speeches of his life, he said, "The commitment of our Fathers is now the calling on our time."[8] This is how he thinks. He could have chosen to see 9/11 as an entirely new struggle in an entirely new day, one in which the founding fathers would be of little use. He chose, instead, to understand the struggle before him as a defense of the commitment of our founding fathers, one that forms a calling on our generation today. The way he understands heritage makes him interpret events this way. It is the lifeblood of his vision, the way he perceives his political task.

Heritage means something very different to Barack Obama. This should not surprise us. Though, like Bush, he has his patriotic family memories—his grandfather served in World War II under George Patton—his heritage leads him to think of America more as something to reform than to preserve. He knows that had his ancestors on his father's side lived in the United States in the early 1800s, they almost certainly would have been slaves. Freedom would have come through courageous political leadership, decisions made in courts, and aggressive social action. None of this is lost on Barack Obama.

His father resisted British rule in Kenya. His mother fought her own counterculture wars in the United States. His childhood world was unique, peopled by freethinkers and filled with an overriding sense that injustice reigns. He concluded that America might one day fulfill its promise but only if it changed.

When Obama came to faith, he was tutored by Rev. Jeremiah Wright. This led him to understand faith as a call to liberation and to liberating work. He clung to Jesus but also to the cause of all who are denied their rights. This sense of mission shaped him as a community organizer, as a lawyer, as a state politician, and ultimately as a US senator and the president of the United States. It is fruit of his faith and the themes within his heritage that faith presses upon him.

Faith aligns the elements of heritage and defines their impact on the soul. It determines the stories to be told, the lessons to be learned. This makes heritage an important factor in any religion, particularly the religions of those who hold political power. Since their duty is to build on what has come before—much in the way a lawyer thinks in terms of case law and precedent—what they believe to be of value in their heritage is of great importance. It can define their sense of mission. It nearly always conditions how they lead.

## Destiny

Most national figures, presidents in particular, possess a strong sense that their ascent to power was predestined. This is usually a product of their religious beliefs. It moves them to view the events of their lives as evidence of a commission, in most cases a divine calling. When this is true of a politician or a president, there are few more important aspects of their faith to explore. The ancient Greeks believed that "character is destiny," but it is also true that what a man or woman believes about his or her destiny is a form of destiny too. It determines much of what he or she becomes.

Winston Churchill is the best example of this. His sense of destiny helped him recover from losses and wounds, gave him courage, and empowered him to inspire his nation. He wrote in his first autobiography, *My Early Life*, about the tension between free will and predestination. He concluded, he said, "that they are identical."[9] It is a statement that can be made only by a man who believes himself chosen, who is confident that his choices fulfill preordained purposes. He believed this of himself completely. As he wrote to his wife from the battlefields of World War I, "Over me beat unseen wings."[10]

He was confident that divine predestination ruled in his life and that it placed him at the helm of the British Empire at the start of World War II. "I felt as if I were walking with destiny," he wrote in his *Second World War*, "and that all my past life had been but a preparation for this hour and for this trial."[11] In the days after, he was frequently able to say of events, "This cannot be accident, it must be design."[12] This article of faith shaped his leadership. It made him courageous, "resolute" he often said. He poured this confidence into his radio broadcasts and public image. It proved a force powerful enough to lift the English people to sacrifice and, in time, to victory.

Presidents often turn to Churchill's example when they ponder their own destiny. They also tend to remember the words of William Shakespeare in *Julius Caesar*.

> There is a tide in the affairs of men,
> Which taken at the flood, leads on to fortune;
> Omitted, all the voyage of their life
> Is bound in shallows and in miseries.
> On such a full sea are we now afloat;
> And we must take the current when it serves,
> Or lose our ventures.[13]

George Washington constantly referred to "Providence" in his correspondence and orders. During the most hellish months at Valley Forge, he wrote of his "indebtedness to Providence" and how the moment had come when "we stand much in need of another manifestation of its bounty however little we deserve it."[14] As president, he relied on "the interposition of Providence."[15]

Abraham Lincoln also felt the hand of destiny. When he was still a teenager, a neighbor woman asked him about his future. "Me?" he replied, "I'm going to be president." A girl close to his age in a nearby town shared his confidence. When her grandmother chastised her for being noisy and asked, "What on earth do you suppose will become of you if you go on this way," the girl responded, "Oh I will be the wife of a president some day."[16] Her name was Mary Todd.

Few presidents have had as clear a sense of divine purpose as George W. Bush. Prior to running for president, Bush met with religious broadcaster James Robison and admitted to a deep sense of urgency: "I can't explain it, but I sense my country is going to need me. Something is going to happen, and, at that time, my country is going to need me. I know it won't be easy, on me or my family, but God wants me to do it."[17]

"In fact," Bush continued, "I really don't want to run. My father was president. My whole family has been affected by it. I know the price. I know what it will mean. I would be perfectly happy to have people point at me someday when I'm buying my fishing lures at Wal-Mart and say, 'That was our governor.' That's all I want. And if I run for president, that kind of life will be over. My life will never be the same. But I know God wants me to do this, and I must do it."[18]

Presidents and those who aspire to the presidency wrestle with questions about calling, about purpose, even about the daunting improbabilities of their story. *Why have I been chosen for this? What is the reason I am here? What lifts one person among three hundred and fifty million to the Oval Office?* They are the kind of questions that look to faith for answers. The heart wants its reason. The mind needs an explanation. There must be some force of fate, some guiding hand, which made their lives turn out as they did. For people of faith, more specifically for people of the Judeo-Christian faith that has guided most of our presidents, divine providence is the answer. Our task is to try to understand what this belief inspires in the soul of the candidate, what it says to them about their past and what it creates in their character.

## The Text

The meaning of a person's faith is usually an extension of how he or she interprets the foundational text of that faith. This may mean, as our postmodern and perhaps post-Christian culture progresses, that we will be required one day to ask how a presidential candidate interprets the Koran or the Bhagavad Gita—perhaps even the Satanic Bible of Anton LaVey. Thus far in American history, however, the foundational text of presidential faith has been the Bible.

This does not mean that all presidents have been orthodox in the way they interpret the Bible. John Kennedy alluded to scripture in his speeches as much as any president in history, yet he routinely applied its meaning to the American experience. In his inaugural address, for example, Kennedy applied Isaiah's admonition—"undo the heavy burdens and to let the oppressed go free"—not to the fasting of righteous Israel but to East-West cooperation during the Cold War.[19] He spoke of a trumpet that summoned Americans to be "rejoicing in hope, patient in tribulation."[20] This technique signaled the centrality of civil religion in Kennedy's thinking, the same civil religion he had expounded in his decisive Houston speech years before.

Barack Obama also takes a nontraditional approach to the Bible. In *The Audacity of Hope*, he described his disagreement with the biblical literalism of men like Ambassador Alan Keyes, Obama's opponent for an Illinois Senate seat. He explained that he was unwilling, for example on the issue of homosexuality, "to accept a reading of the Bible that considers an obscure line in Romans to be more defining of Christianity than the Sermon on the Mount."[21] This granting of authority to one verse from the Bible over another was a break from traditional Christianity, and Obama knew it. He was identifying himself as a theological liberal whose view of scripture bolstered his progressive politics. "When I read the Bible," he wrote in 2006, "I do so with the belief that it is not a static text but the Living Word and that I must be continually open to new revelations—whether they come from a lesbian friend or a doctor opposed to abortion."[22]

Almost every faith requires the faithful to interact with the written word, with documents of faith handed down. Normally, the way they go about this determines what kind of believer they will be. For people in political leadership, this is a particularly important issue, for there is commonly a connection between their approach to their religious text and their approach to their political purpose. The one feeds the other; the hermeneutic or interpretive approach to the one becomes the method of deciding the other. Some scholars suggest that there is even a connection between the way some politicians approach their Bibles and the way they approach the Constitution. It can distinguish the two sides of the political aisle, the conservative from the progressive. It reflects the divide between the religious traditionalist and the theological modernist.

What is certain is that a person's faith is determined by how he or she interprets the text at the foundation of that faith. This relationship between believer and text is an interaction to watch carefully and to question respectfully. The answers to these questions, if truthful, should anticipate much of what the person will become.

## The Clergy

An obvious indicator of a president's faith and his direction in office is his interaction with religious leaders. Clergy are ever present in a president's life. They lead worship services, say prayers at the start of every kind of event, represent their communities at policy meetings, and give their opinion directly and indirectly on nearly everything a president does. How a president perceives them, how he interacts with them, what access he grants them, and what influence they have on him are all important factors to consider.

Of the hundreds of clergy a president knows, usually only a few will become part of his inner circle. These will likely leave a lasting imprint, though. Even if the relationship between preacher and president is rocky, it is still revealing and so helps us learn the possible impact of faith upon the chief executive's politics.

From the beginning, clergymen shaped the views of presidents. This was a natural extension of the times. Clergymen were among the most influential figures in early American society. Many of them led units in the Revolutionary War, and some were part of the conventions that crafted the founding documents of the nation. Even apart from these roles, ministers in that era were a combination of today's megachurch pastor, university president, political party chief, and Oprah Winfrey. For many of the more prominent pastors in early America, to speak to a president was to speak to a peer, nearly an equal, so great was their standing in society.

Some of this esteem for clergy came from the high regard Americans had for George Whitefield. He is usually remembered in our textbooks as the Anglican priest who led a series of religious revivals from Georgia to Maine. In doing this, though, his crusades became the first "intercolonial event"—a unifying force among the otherwise disconnected colonies. He used the force of his fame to warn the colonists about the designs against them being fashioned by the British Crown and Parliament. Speaking to an assembly of fellow ministers at Portsmouth in 1764, a tearful Whitefield sounded the alarm.

> I can't in conscience leave the town without acquainting you with a secret. My heart bleeds for America. O poor New England! There is a deep laid plot against both your civil and religious liberties, and they will be lost. Your golden days are at an end. You have nothing but trouble before you.[23]

His predictions of golden days at an end were overstated, of course, but the founding generation revered Whitefield both for his spiritual ministry and for his concern for their liberty.

Colonial era clergymen like Whitefield assured that government officials would welcome the counsel of religious leaders for generations to come. This continued in Abraham Lincoln's years. Though many preachers suspected Lincoln, who had been an outspoken religious skeptic in his early life and had never joined a church, he welcomed them openly. One man in particular made a decisive difference in Lincoln's life. His name was Dr. Francis Vinton, pastor of Trinity

Episcopal Church on Broadway in New York City. His visit with Lincoln occurred two weeks after Willie Lincoln, the president's beloved son, had died. Since that time, Lincoln—who had fought depression all his life and several times contemplated suicide—had locked himself in a dark room one day a week to grieve. When Dr. Vinton heard of this, he made an appointment to see the president. A painter named F. B. Carpenter, who was working in the White House at the time, recorded what occurred.

> He [Vinton] told him [Lincoln] plainly that the indulgence of such feelings, though natural, was sinful. It was unworthy of one who believed in the Christian religion. He had duties to the living, greater than those of any other man, as the chosen father, and leader of the people, and he was unfitting himself for his responsibilities by thus giving way to his grief. To mourn the departed as *lost* belonged to heathenism—not to Christianity. "Your son," said Dr. Vinton, "is alive, in Paradise. Do you remember that passage in the Gospels: 'God is not the God of the dead but of the living, for all live unto him'?"
>
> The President had listened as one in a stupor, until his ear caught the words, "Your son is alive." Starting from the sofa, he exclaimed, "Alive! *alive!* Surely you mock me." "No, sir, believe me," replied Dr. Vinton; "it is a most comforting doctrine of the church founded upon the words of Christ himself."
>
> Mr. Lincoln looked at him a moment, then, stepping forward, he threw his arm around the clergyman's neck, and, laying his head upon his breast, sobbed aloud. "Alive? alive?" he repeated. "My dear sir," said Dr. Vinton, greatly moved, as he twined his own arm around the weeping father, "believe this, for it is God's most precious truth. Seek not your son among the dead; he is not there; he lives to-day in Paradise."

Vinton then proceeded to cite scripture in support of his message, and after referring particularly to the words of Jesus and Jacob, he said:

189

And so God has called your son into his upper kingdom—a kingdom and an existence as real, more real, than your own. It may be that he too, like Joseph, has gone, in God's good providence, to be the salvation of his father's household.

Finally, Vinton offered, "I have a sermon upon this subject, which I think might interest you." Mr. Lincoln begged him to send it at an early day—thanking him repeatedly for his cheering and hopeful words. The sermon was sent, and read over and over by the President, who caused a copy to be made for his own private use before it was returned. Through a member of the family, I [Carpenter] have been informed that Mr. Lincoln's views in relation to spiritual things seemed changed from that hour.[24]

Clergymen would continue to press into presidents' lives for decades more. Not all meetings would go as well as Dr. Vinton's with Abraham Lincoln. One in particular was a disaster.

When Billy Graham was just gaining notoriety, he asked to visit with President Harry Truman. The two men met at the White House in 1950. Graham was intense, sincere, and naïve. He talked with Truman—a nominal Baptist at best—about the need for the gospel in America and asked if he could lead a prayer. Truman agreed. Graham prayed, shook Truman's hand, and left.

As the evangelist walked out of the White House, an eager band of newspapermen and photographers surrounded him. When Graham told them about the prayer, they asked him to reenact it. The newspapermen knew what they were doing. Graham did not. Thinking he was modeling prayer for the nation, Graham knelt on the White House lawn and re-prayed. Photos of the scene hit the front pages of the nation's newspapers the next day. Truman was incensed. Graham apologized and through the years spoke often of the embarrassing episode as a warning to other ministers of influence in politics.

In more recent history, ministers have sometimes been as influential in policy matters as they have long been in spiritual concerns. Ronald

Reagan met often with leaders of the newly formed Religious Right, men like D. James Kennedy, Jerry Falwell, and James Robison. Each of them spoke to policy matters, and some served on federal boards and committees. The Clintons also welcomed a huge variety of religious leaders to White House events, clearly hoping to forge a new consensus or craft a new unity among the nation's leading spiritual voices. This led to Hillary Clinton's embarrassing meeting with Jean Houston, a meeting some later called the "Séance in the Solarium."

George W. Bush took counsel from a wide variety of pastors and religious leaders. James Robison, the man to whom he first confessed his sense of a call to run for office, routinely provided input on policy matters, as did others whose views Bush respected. Some of these regularly sent their thoughts directly to a fax machine in the West Wing.

Barack Obama was equally attentive to the counsel of ministers, though events just before he entered office left him with a far more diverse group of spiritual advisors than most presidents allow. After the famous break with Rev. Jeremiah Wright during the 2008 campaign, the Obama family found themselves without a pastor just as they were moving into the White House. Joshua DuBois, who had headed faith outreach for the Obama campaign and was soon to be director of the Office of Faith-Based and Community Initiatives, asked the new president if he would welcome a team of spiritual advisors. Obama said he would. DuBois formed a group of leading ministers that included evangelical pastor Joel Hunter; African American church leaders T. D. Jakes, Kirbyjon Caldwell, and T. Otis Moss; and *Sojourners* magazine founder, Jim Wallis, among others.

These men met as they could with Obama for prayer. Conference calls better suited the president's schedule and during these the team of ministers would challenge Obama, probe him about spiritual matters, and pray for his needs. They also sometimes gave input on broader religious matters, and some even advised on less-faith-based

191

issues. They went so far as to write devotionals for Obama. These were sent to DuBois, who edited them and forwarded them daily to the president's BlackBerry. DuBois later formed these devotionals into a bestselling book, *The President's Devotional: The Daily Readings That Inspired President Obama.*

During these years, Obama was spiritually a work in progress. He had known only Jeremiah Wright as his pastor prior to becoming president. This left him with a heightened social conscience but without the kind of grounding in scripture and Christian theology he might have received from a less activist church. Through the mentoring of his spiritual advisors, he began to get his questions answered, started to acquire a deeper connection to Jesus Christ and the Bible. Still, his political worldview had not absorbed the full meaning of the truth he was receiving, had not undergone the same transformation as his heart through the ministry of his dutiful spiritual advisors.

This meant there were surprises. When Obama changed his mind about same-sex marriage, Joel Hunter was stunned. And disappointed. Obama had come into office a supporter of traditional marriage. He and Hunter had often discussed the biblical basis for this view. Yet suddenly, without discussing the matter with Hunter, Obama changed his mind and attributed the reversal to Christ's teaching on the Golden Rule in the Sermon on the Mount.

Just before *ABC News* was scheduled to air a broadcast announcing Obama's shift in view, the president called the pastor. He knew Hunter would be disappointed, but he called out of respect and to preserve the friendship. Hunter, always a shepherd but never a man to soften the truth, replied that he disagreed with the president's position and that this reversal would make it harder for him to support him. Obama said he understood and that he would protect the religious freedom of churches that oppose gay marriage.[25]

The tensions between the two men on the matter of same-sex marriage illustrate the way it often is in the relationships between presidents and the religious leaders who advise them. There are disagreements. There are often disappointments. Yet this is natural—even healthy—and it is a part of a president's faith life that tells us much about his thinking on religious matters, the condition of his soul, and the imprint both of these will have on the way he leads the nation. We need not be suspicious of religious leaders influencing politicians, but we do need to be attentive if we hope to understand the broader matter of how religion will shape the presidency.

## The Political Theology

When a person of faith enters politics, he brings with him all he believes. His religion will be a part of this but not all of it. The ideas of his faith will blend with his political and economic ideas, and these may become one with the certainties he has acquired from all his experience, all he has read, and all he has been told by those he respects.

It will all form, ultimately, into a political theology, a faith-informed body of beliefs that will shape all he does in office. If we want to understand any political leader who leans to religion in what he or she does, we should always be in pursuit of understanding this political theology. It forms part of the intellectual capital of presidential leaders, as we've seen Henry Kissinger explain. It crafts the lens through which a president views the world. It creates the context of values and morals in which decisions are made. In short, it counsels the president in all he does. The philosopher George Santayana believed that this is religion's proper role.

> It should be observed that, if a systematic religion is true at all, intrusion on its part into politics is not only legitimate, but is the very work it comes into the world to do. Being by hypothesis, enlightened supernaturally, it is able to survey the conditions and consequences of any kind of action much better than the wisest legislature . . .

193

so that spheres of systematic religion and politics—far from being independent are in principle identical.[26]

This is how most presidents who are sincere about their faith think about the counsel of religion in what they do. They may not want to admit it publicly. They may not want it to become part of their public brand. Yet what Santayana describes is exactly what a deeply faith-based president wants his religion to do.

We should be careful, though, not to expect presidents to think like theologians, not to expect complex systems of belief. A political theology can be drawn from a single sentence. It can be captured from a story or in some cases even a phrase. What is important is not the extent of the language. What is important is the influence of an idea or a belief on the political behavior of the individual. A political theology is simply a religious idea or a series of ideas that influences political action.

Though Hillary Clinton is not an American president, we have seen that a single sentence has formed most of her political theology. Her mentor, Don Jones, pressed into her young mind the single truth that had changed his own life: "Christianity is a faith that either relieves the suffering of others or is dead."

If Clinton believes this, then it explains the political vision she has drawn from it. It explains why, for her, political action is largely a matter of finding the hurting and the disenfranchised and using the powers of state to relieve their condition. This helps us understand the reason she has been at her fiercest in defending women's rights, in seeking equality for gays, in arguing her view of immigration, in increasing welfare benefits for the poor, and in working for economic equality in America. She understands politics in the same way she understands the Methodist purpose in the 1700s. She taught often that John Wesley "preached a gospel of social justice demanding as determinedly as ever that society do right by all its people."

Barack Obama's political theology is not far from Clinton's. Having looked to Jeremiah Wright for the biblical references to undergird his progressive politics, he absorbed the feel if not all the content of Wright's liberation theology.

This understanding of the Christian gospel is rooted in a vision of Jesus Christ as a liberator of humanity. Since Jesus described himself as a liberator—whose task was to "proclaim good news to the poor . . . to proclaim freedom for the prisoners . . . to set the oppressed free"—the work of God's faithful now ought to be the same.[27] The intellectual father of Wright's black liberation theology was James Cone. He taught that the work of liberation—political, economic, social, and, yes, religious—was the work of God. As he said, "In a word, God's revelation means liberation—nothing more, nothing less."[28]

Obama would not use this language. It is too incendiary, too easily misunderstood. Yet he came to political leadership armed with a belief that religion had been used by conservatives to urge the wrong things in American society. Obama saw in the pages of his Bible a different set of values that would lead to a different America. As he said to a convention of his own United Church of Christ denomination in 2007:

> Somehow, somewhere along the way, faith stopped being used to bring us together and started being used to drive us apart. It got hijacked. Part of it's because of the so-called leaders of the Christian Right, who've been all too eager to exploit what divides us. At every opportunity, they've told evangelical Christians that Democrats disrespect their values and dislike their Church, while suggesting to the rest of the country that religious Americans care only about issues like abortion and gay marriage; school prayer and intelligent design. There was even a time when the Christian Coalition determined that its number one legislative priority was tax cuts for the rich. I don't know what Bible they're reading, but it doesn't jibe with my version.[29]

Obama's political theology is, like Clinton's, rooted in a sense of divine call to liberate the oppressed, to do the work of Christ the liberator. It is why he cites the Golden Rule from the Sermon on the Mount on behalf of same-sex marriage. It is why he finds it difficult to stray very far from the Palestinian cause. It is the reason he works for a state health care system and open immigration and unrestricted abortion rights. For him, each of these issues is about a people being oppressed. His faith demands he do what he can to liberate them. The work of the state must be the work of God.

George W. Bush came to political leadership armed with an equally unique blend of ideas. He had absorbed from Ronald Reagan and his father the belief that American government was failing because it had become bloated, overreaching, fiscally irresponsible, and often corrupt. He was fully convinced that the answers for these maladies could be found in traditional American civic wisdom: a decentralized government, low taxes, a strong defense, the rule of law, and clear, constitutional boundaries.

He was also influenced by a new breed of Christian thinkers. One of the most important to Bush's understanding of faith-based politics was Marvin Olasky, a University of Texas professor who had converted from Marxism to evangelical Christianity. Olasky had written *The Tragedy of American Compassion*, which argued that the American war on poverty had made poverty worse, that government is not the answer, that social solutions have often been crafted by religious organizations, and that the time had come for an unleashing of that force for good once again.

Bush drank deeply of Olasky's vision and began calling for faith-based institutions to reform society and for larded state and federal bureaucracies to get out of the way. By 1995, Bush was governor of Texas and aflame with this new cause. Olasky himself chronicled Bush's firestorm of initiatives in a journal article he wrote at the time.

He issued an Executive Order making Texas the first state to establish the option of using private and religious charities to deliver welfare services. He set up a level playing field for both religious and nonreligious groups for Texas social service contracts, abstinence education grants, and poverty-fighting initiatives. He made Texas the first state to permit a state prison unit to be operated by a ministry. He established alternative licensing procedures for many faith-based programs. He created a pilot program establishing Second Chance group homes for unwed teen welfare mothers run by faith-based and other private groups. He proposed and signed a Good Samaritan law that gives liability protection to health professionals who donate charitable care to needy Texans. He recommended and signed a law requiring governmental agencies to develop welfare-to-work partnerships with faith-based groups in a way that respects those groups' unique religious character.[30]

Bush had become convinced that the US government was too big, too uncaring, too secular, and too entrenched. His answer was "compassionate conservatism," a reversal of the trends that had siphoned off American greatness. "Government can do certain things very well," Bush said at the time, "but it cannot put hope in our hearts or a sense of purpose in our lives."[31] His political theology, then, was built upon the principles of American exceptionalism and the principles of faith-based social action as articulated by Marvin Olasky. All of this was fueled by his confidence in a destiny-weaving God. As he wrote at the time, "I could not be governor if I did not believe in a divine plan that supersedes all human plans."[32]

For those who had been watching Bush closely, what he became as president was a natural outgrowth of what he had come to believe—about God, about the past, about his own calling, and about the best tactics for social change—before he ever considered running for the Oval Office. This is because his political theology had already taken shape years before, and this is, as Kissinger reminded us, true of all presidents. The beliefs that have congealed in their minds before taking office are what they will use to lead. It cannot be otherwise. The presidency allows little time to reflect and less time to learn. Presidents usually leave office with the same religious beliefs and thus with the same political theology they held on the day of their inauguration. Our goal must be to discern this theology's dimensions and implications based on the portion of it we are allowed to see.

These, then, are essential features of the narrative of faith we hope will fully form in our minds about every candidate we must ever consider. There are other features, of course. One concerns the manner in which a person relies on faith to help them navigate through the worst crises of their life. Another is how faith defines ethics and how it safeguards moral conduct. These are important facets of a life of faith. We should strive to know them if we can. Yet they are such internal and personal matters that we often will not be granted access. This is particularly true with politicians, most of whom cherish privacy, some of whom are not reflective enough to know themselves, and all of whom manage their stories to create the desired effect. We have to accept that there are aspects of candidates' faiths we will never be allowed to know.

Yet we must never hesitate to ask the question. This chapter begins with an odd quote. It is a statement Adolf Hitler made in *Mein Kampf*: "I believe today that my conduct is in accordance with the will of the Almighty Creator." He was in prison and largely unknown when he wrote these words. Years later this single sentence thrilled Hitler's audiences. It adorned posters, was a refrain in his speeches, and was often heard breathlessly recited by Hitler Youth.

Yet the German people at that time, very much like us today, rarely understood the whole. They did not know the story, the narrative arc, the pillars of Hitler's life and faith. If they had, they might have realized that he used his religion and his church as a disguise for evils from which we are still laboring to recover. The completion of that sentence in *Mein Kampf* anticipated the horrors yet to come: "By defending myself against the Jew, I am fighting for the work of the Lord."[33]

Knowing only in bits and pieces blinds us to the whole. We must learn the stories of faith before we grant power to candidates for high office. What is vague in a campaign may become pronounced once the candidate is in power. Our goal is to limit unpleasant surprises.

# Epilogue

I know no safe depository of the ultimate powers of the society but the people themselves.

Thomas Jefferson

We live in a world even the experts struggle to define. We feel along its edges. We know it rockets forward, forcing changes almost beyond our comprehension. We know that many cultures, languages, religions, and ethnicities throng before us. We find ourselves both rooted in the moment and living almost timeless technological lives, both tethered to the local and yet citizens of something new and global that seems to expand dramatically nearly every minute.

This new, indefinable world has changed the matrix of religions in our lives. We might know what we believe. We might have found the faith that feels to us like home. Yet it does not reduce the religious complexity in which we live. We must contend every day with faiths that are new to us and also with faiths that are customized and individualized by the people we know and love.

You have a friend who calls himself an agnostic. He comes to lunch excited about something he heard in a podcast by T. D. Jakes. He is going to hear the Dalai Llama lecture next week. That Deepak

Chopra special on National Public Television pulled him from his slump last year. He's grateful. Tonight his yoga class is going together to the Joel Osteen "Your Best Life Now" event at the arena. He wonders if you'll go too.

Another friend is Roman Catholic and is always talking about her priest. She says Father Shawn and Jack Black were separated at birth. She arrives for drinks tanned from hiking Machu Picchu in Peru, where she attended a meditation seminar while sitting on stones placed by Incas centuries ago. She is a tech firm executive who is both eager to be a success and eager to make a difference in the world. She won't miss a Tony Robbins seminar and joins Heal the Earth overseas teams every year. She interned on Capitol Hill in college and worked in Appalachia with Habitat for Humanity for a year after she earned her master's at the Kennedy School at Harvard. She is one to watch—if you can keep up.

You know a hundred like them. We all do. It is the way of things these days.

Now, suppose someone like them runs for president. You have to decide how to vote. So you take a long look at the candidates. You examine their experience, their positions on issues, how they carry themselves in debates, what they have done in leadership positions before, and even their financial statements and tax returns. With each of them, a patchwork of religions and spiritual experiences is important. It is part of who they are, part of what they constantly mention in speeches. You even notice a diverse series of religious leaders who meet with them, who are sometimes standing with them on TV.

You realize you have to drill down into their spirituality. You can't honestly vote until you know what they believe or at least who will influence them religiously while in office. There is no campaign literature, no YouTube video, no single blog that says it all in one place. You have to piece together an understanding of their faith. You have to ask questions. You have to let an overall story or narrative form in your mind. It is the only way you will ever be able to vote and feel good about it, to know you've done what every voter should do.

Then you hear that the candidate you are leaning toward is speaking at an open forum nearby. You have to be there. That night you get a good seat, listen to the opening comments, and are ready when the time for questions comes.

Several others talk, and then the moderator points to you. A techie puts a microphone in your hand. You rise, turn fully to the candidate, and take a breath. You choose a question from the list in your mind, the one that is most likely to draw the candidate out on the spirituality he says is important to him but for you is yet unclear.

Now it comes. The moment clarity can dawn. It only comes, though, if you will boldly ask the question.

# Three Speeches

There are three seminal presidential speeches about the role of religion in American politics that are essential reading for all who wish to understand this issue well. John F. Kennedy's 1960 Houston speech was designed to deal with his "Catholic problem" and became one of the premiere statements of American civil religion. Ronald Reagan's 1984 "Remarks at a Dallas Ecumenical Prayer Breakfast" was typical of many such talks that he gave and captured what might be called a "covenantal" approach to religion and politics. This is the view that all Americans are involved in a commission from God by virtue of their American citizenship. Barack Obama's 2006 "Call to Renewal" speech is one of the clearest affirmations of religion's proper role in the American public square yet with deference to pluralism and secularism. Together, these speeches provide an essential overview of the perspectives that have prevailed in recent decades, but they also provide something of a survey of themes that have surfaced repeatedly throughout American history.

# John F. Kennedy's Speech to the Greater Houston Ministerial Association

Rice Hotel, Houston, Texas
September 12, 1960

Rev. Meza, Rev. Reck, I'm grateful for your generous invitation to speak my views.

While the so-called religious issue is necessarily and properly the chief topic here tonight, I want to emphasize from the outset that we have far more critical issues to face in the 1960 election: the spread of communist influence, until it now festers ninety miles off the coast of Florida; the humiliating treatment of our president and vice president by those who no longer respect our power; the hungry children I saw in West Virginia; the old people who cannot pay their doctor bills; the families forced to give up their farms; an America with too many slums, with too few schools, and too late to the moon and outer space.

These are the real issues that should decide this campaign. And they are not religious issues—for war and hunger and ignorance and despair know no religious barriers.

But because I am a Catholic, and no Catholic has ever been elected president, the real issues in this campaign have been obscured—perhaps deliberately in some quarters less responsible than this. So it is apparently necessary for me to state once again not what kind of church I believe in—for that should be important only to me—but what kind of America I believe in.

I believe in an America where the separation of church and state is absolute, where no Catholic prelate would tell the president (should he be Catholic) how to act, and no Protestant minister would tell his parishioners for whom to vote; where no church or church school is granted any public funds or political preference; and where no man is denied public office merely because his religion differs from the president who might appoint him or the people who might elect him.

I believe in an America that is officially neither Catholic, Protestant, nor Jewish; where no public official either requests or accepts instructions on public policy from the pope, the National Council of Churches, or any other ecclesiastical source; where no religious body seeks to impose its will directly or indirectly upon the general populace or the public acts of its officials; and where religious liberty is so indivisible that an act against one church is treated as an act against all.

For while this year it may be a Catholic against whom the finger of suspicion is pointed, in other years it has been, and may someday be again, a Jew—or a Quaker or a Unitarian or a Baptist. It was Virginia's harassment of Baptist preachers, for example, that helped lead to Jefferson's Statute of Religious Freedom. Today I may be the victim, but tomorrow it may be you—until the whole fabric of our harmonious society is ripped at a time of great national peril.

Finally, I believe in an America where religious intolerance will someday end; where all men and all churches are treated as equal; where every man has the same right to attend or not attend the church of his choice; where there is no Catholic vote, no anti-Catholic vote, no bloc voting of any kind; and where Catholics, Protestants, and Jews, at both the lay and pastoral level, will refrain from those attitudes of disdain and division which have so often marred their works in the past and promote instead the American ideal of brotherhood.

That is the kind of America in which I believe. And it represents the kind of presidency in which I believe—a great office that must neither be humbled by making it the instrument of any one religious group nor tarnished by arbitrarily withholding its occupancy from the members of any one religious group. I believe in a president whose religious views are his own private affair, neither imposed by him upon the nation or imposed by the nation upon him as a condition to holding that office.

I would not look with favor upon a president working to subvert the First Amendment's guarantees of religious liberty. Nor would our system of checks and balances permit him to do so. And neither do I look with favor upon those who would work to subvert Article VI of the Constitution by requiring a religious test—even by indirection—for it. If they disagree with that safeguard, they should be out openly working to repeal it.

I want a chief executive whose public acts are responsible to all groups and obligated to none; who can attend any ceremony, service, or dinner his office may appropriately require of him; and whose fulfillment of his presidential oath is not limited or conditioned by any religious oath, ritual, or obligation.

This is the kind of America I believe in, and this is the kind I fought for in the South Pacific, and the kind my brother died for in Europe. No one suggested then that we may have a "divided loyalty," that we did "not believe in liberty," or that we belonged to a disloyal group that threatened the "freedoms for which our forefathers died."

And in fact, this is the kind of America for which our forefathers died, when they fled here to escape religious test oaths that denied office to members of less favored churches; when they fought for the Constitution, the Bill of Rights, and the Virginia Statute of Religious Freedom; and when they fought at the shrine I visited today, the Alamo. For side by side with Bowie and Crockett died McCafferty and Bailey and Carey. But no one knows whether they were Catholic or not, for there was no religious test at the Alamo.

I ask you tonight to follow in that tradition, to judge me on the basis of my record of fourteen years in Congress, on my declared stands against an ambassador to the Vatican, against unconstitutional aid to parochial schools, and against any boycott of the public schools (which I have attended myself)—instead of judging me on the basis of these pamphlets and publications we all have seen that carefully select quotations out of context from the statements of Catholic church leaders, usually in other countries, frequently in other centuries, and always omitting, of course, the statement of the American bishops in 1948, which strongly endorsed church-state separation and which more nearly reflects the views of almost every American Catholic.

I do not consider these other quotations binding upon my public acts. Why should you? But let me say, with respect to other countries, that I am wholly opposed to the state being used by any religious group, Catholic or Protestant, to compel, prohibit, or persecute the free exercise of any other religion. And I hope that you and I condemn with equal fervor those nations which deny their presidency to Protestants, and those which deny it to Catholics. And rather than cite the misdeeds of those who differ, I would cite the record of the Catholic Church in such nations as Ireland and France and the independence of such statesmen as Adenauer and De Gaulle.

But let me stress again that these are my views. For contrary to common newspaper usage, I am not the Catholic candidate for president. I am the Democratic Party's candidate for president who happens also to be a Catholic. I do not speak for my church on public matters, and the church does not speak for me.

Whatever issue may come before me as president—on birth control, divorce, censorship, gambling, or any other subject—I will make my decision in accordance with these views, in accordance with what my conscience tells me to be the national interest, and without regard to outside religious pressures or dictates. And no power or threat of punishment could cause me to decide otherwise.

But if the time should ever come—and I do not concede any conflict to be even remotely possible—when my office would require me to either violate my conscience or violate the national interest, then I would resign the office, and I hope any conscientious public servant would do the same.

But I do not intend to apologize for these views to my critics of either Catholic or Protestant faith, nor do I intend to disavow either my views or my church in order to win this election.

If I should lose on the real issues, I shall return to my seat in the Senate, satisfied that I had tried my best and was fairly judged. But if this election is decided on the basis that forty million Americans lost their chance of being president on the day they were baptized, then it is the whole nation that will be the loser—in the eyes of Catholics and non-Catholics around the world, in the eyes of history, and in the eyes of our own people.

But if, on the other hand, I should win the election, then I shall devote every effort of mind and spirit to fulfilling the oath of the presidency—practically identical, I might add, to the oath I have taken for fourteen years in the Congress. For without reservation, I can "solemnly swear that I will faithfully execute the office of president of the United States, and will to the best of my ability preserve, protect, and defend the Constitution, so help me God."

# Ronald Reagan's "Remarks at a Dallas Ecumenical Prayer Breakfast"

Reunion Arena, Dallas, Texas
August 23, 1984

Thank you very much. Thank you, ladies and gentlemen, very much. And, Martha Weisend, thank you very much. And I could say that if the morning ended with the music we have just heard from that magnificent choir, it would indeed be a holy day for all of us.

It's wonderful to be here this morning. The past few days have been busy for all of us, but I wanted to be with you today to share some of my own thoughts.

These past few weeks it seems that we've all been hearing a lot of talk about religion and its role in politics, religion and its place in the political life of the nation. And I think it's appropriate today, at a prayer breakfast for seventeen thousand citizens in the state of Texas during a great political convention, that this issue be addressed.

I don't speak as a theologian or a scholar, only as one who's lived a little more than his threescore ten—which has—which has been a source of annoyance to some—and as one who has been active in the political life of the nation for roughly four decades and now who's served the past three and a half years in our highest office. I speak, I think I can say, as one who has seen much, who has loved his country, and who's seen it change in many ways.

213

I believe that faith and religion play a critical role in the political life of our nation, and always have, and that the church—and by that I mean all churches, all denominations—has had a strong influence on the state, and this has worked to our benefit as a nation.

Those who created our country—the founding fathers and mothers—understood that there is a divine order which transcends the human order. They saw the state, in fact, as a form of moral order and felt that the bedrock of moral order is religion.

The Mayflower Compact began with the words, "In the name of God, Amen." The Declaration of Independence appeals to "Nature's God" and the "Creator" and "the Supreme Judge of the world." Congress was given a chaplain, and the oaths of office are oaths before God.

James Madison in *The Federalist Papers* admitted that in the creation of our republic he perceived the hand of the Almighty. John Jay, the first chief justice of the Supreme Court, warned that we must never forget the God from whom our blessings flowed.

George Washington referred to religion's profound and unsurpassed place in the heart of our nation quite directly in his Farewell Address in 1796. Seven years earlier, France had erected a government that was intended to be purely secular. This new government would be grounded on reason rather than the law of God. By 1796, the French Revolution had known the Reign of Terror.

And Washington voiced reservations about the idea that there could be a wise policy without a firm moral and religious foundation. He said, "Of all the dispositions and habits which lead to political prosperity, religion and morality are indispensable supports. In vain would that man (call himself a patriot) who (would) labor to subvert these . . . finest props of the duties of men and citizens. The mere politician . . . (and) the pious man ought to respect and to cherish (religion and morality)." And he added, "Let us with caution indulge the supposition that morality can be maintained without religion." I believe that George Washington knew the city of man cannot survive without the city of God, that the—that the visible city will perish without the invisible city.

Religion played not only a strong role in our national life, it played a positive role. The abolitionist movement was at heart a moral and religious movement; so was the modern civil rights struggle. And throughout this time, the state was tolerant of religious belief, expression, and practice. Society, too, was tolerant.

But in the 1960s, this began to change. We began to make great steps toward secularizing our nation and removing religion from its honored place. In 1962, the Supreme Court, in the New York prayer case, banned the compulsory saying of prayers. In 1963, the court banned the reading of the Bible in our public schools. From that point on, the courts pushed the meaning of the ruling ever outward so that now our children are not allowed voluntary prayer. We even had to pass a law—we passed a special law in the Congress just a few weeks ago—to allow student prayer groups the same access to schoolrooms after classes that a young Marxist society, for example, would already enjoy with no opposition.

The 1962 decision opened the way to a flood of similar suits. Once religion had been made vulnerable, a series of assaults were made in one court after another, on one issue after another. Cases were started to argue against tax-exempt status for churches. Suits were brought to abolish the words "under God" from the Pledge of Allegiance and to remove "in God we trust" from public documents and from our currency.

Today there are those who are fighting to make sure voluntary prayer is not returned to the classrooms. And the frustrating thing for the great majority of Americans who support and understand the special importance of religion in the national life—the frustrating thing is that those who are attacking religion claim they are doing it in the name of tolerance, freedom, and open-mindedness. Question:

215

Isn't the real truth that they are intolerant of religion? They refuse to tolerate its importance in our lives.

If all the children of our country studied together all of the many religions in our country, wouldn't they learn greater tolerance of each other's beliefs? If children prayed together, would they not understand what they have in common? And would this not, indeed, bring them closer? And is this not to be desired? So I submit to you that those who claim to be fighting for tolerance on this issue may not be tolerant at all.

When John Kennedy was running for president in 1960, he said that his church would not dictate his presidency any more than he would speak for his church. Just so, and proper. But John Kennedy was speaking in an America in which the role of religion—and by that I mean the role of all churches—was secure. Abortion was not a political issue. Prayer was not a political issue. The right of church schools to operate was not a political issue. And it was broadly acknowledged that religious leaders had a right and a duty to speak out on the issues of the day. They held a place of respect, and a politician who spoke to or of them with a lack of respect would not long survive in the political arena. It was acknowledged then that religion held a special place, occupied a special territory in the hearts of the citizenry. The climate has changed greatly since then. And since it has, it logically follows that religion needs defenders against those who care only for the interests of the state.

There are, these days, many questions on which religious leaders are obliged to offer their moral and theological guidance, and such guidance is a good and necessary thing. To know how a church and its members feel on a public issue expands the parameters of debate. It does not narrow the debate; it expands it.

The truth is politics and morality are inseparable. And—and as morality's foundation is religion, religion and politics are necessarily related. We need religion as a guide. We need it because we are

216

imperfect, and our government needs the church because only those humble enough to admit they're sinners can bring to democracy the tolerance it requires in order to survive.

A state is nothing more than a reflection of its citizens: The more decent the citizens, the more decent the state. If you practice a religion, whether you're Catholic, Protestant, Jewish, or guided by some other faith, then your private life will be influenced by a sense of moral obligation, and so, too, will your public life. One affects the other. The churches of America do not exist by the grace of the state; the churches of America are not mere citizens of the state. The churches of America exist apart; they have their own vantage point, their own authority. Religion is its own realm; it makes its own claims.

We establish no religion in this country, nor will we ever. We command no worship. We mandate no belief. But we poison our society when we remove its theological underpinnings. We court corruption when we leave it bereft of belief. All are free to believe or not to believe; all are free to practice a faith or not. But those who believe must be free to speak of and act on their belief, to apply moral teaching to public questions.

I submit to you that the tolerant society is open to and encouraging of all religions. And this does not weaken us; it strengthens us; it makes us strong. You know, if we look back through history to all those great civilizations, those great nations that rose up to even world dominance and then deteriorated, declined, and fell, we find they all had one thing in common. One of the significant forerunners of their fall was their turning away from their God or gods.

Without God, there is no virtue, because there's no prompting of the conscience. Without God, we're mired in the material, that flat world that tells us only what the senses perceive. Without God, there is a coarsening of the society. And without God, democracy will not and cannot long endure. If we ever forget that we're one nation under God, then we will be a nation gone under.

If I could just make a personal statement of my own: In these three and a half years, I have understood and known better than ever before the words of Lincoln, when he said that he would be the greatest fool on this footstool called earth if he ever thought that for one moment he could perform the duties of that office without help from One who is stronger than all.

I thank you, thank you for inviting us here today. Thank you for your kindness and your patience. May God keep you, and we—may we, all of us, keep God.

Thank you.

# Barack Obama's "Call to Renewal" Speech

Building a Covenant for a New America Conference
Washington, DC
June 28, 2006

Good morning. I appreciate the opportunity to speak here at the Call to Renewal's Building a Covenant for a New America Conference. I've had the opportunity to take a look at your Covenant for a New America. It is filled with outstanding policies and prescriptions for much of what ails this country. So I'd like to congratulate you all on the thoughtful presentations you've given so far about poverty and justice in America, and for putting fire under the feet of the political leadership here in Washington.

But today I'd like to talk about the connection between religion and politics and perhaps offer some thoughts about how we can sort through some of the often bitter arguments that we've been seeing over the last several years.

I do so because, as you all know, we can affirm the importance of poverty in the Bible, and we can raise up and pass out this Covenant for a New America. We can talk to the press, and we can discuss the religious call to address poverty and environmental stewardship all we want, but it won't have an impact unless we tackle head-on the mutual suspicion that sometimes exists between religious America and secular America.

I want to give you an example that I think illustrates this fact. As some of you know, during the 2004 US Senate general election, I ran against a gentleman named Alan Keyes. Mr. Keyes is well-versed in the Jerry Falwell–Pat Robertson style of rhetoric that often labels progressives as both immoral and godless.

Indeed, Mr. Keyes announced toward the end of the campaign that "Jesus Christ would not vote for Barack Obama. Christ would not vote for Barack Obama because Barack Obama has behaved in a way that it is inconceivable for Christ to have behaved."

Jesus Christ would not vote for Barack Obama.

Now, I was urged by some of my liberal supporters not to take this statement seriously, to essentially ignore it. To them, Mr. Keyes was an extremist and his arguments not worth entertaining. And since at the time I was up forty points in the polls, it probably wasn't a bad piece of strategic advice.

But what they didn't understand, however, was that I had to take Mr. Keyes seriously, for he claimed to speak for my religion and my God. He claimed knowledge of certain truths.

Mr. Obama says he's a Christian, he was saying, and yet he supports a lifestyle that the Bible calls an abomination.

Mr. Obama says he's a Christian but supports the destruction of innocent and sacred life.

And so what would my supporters have me say? How should I respond? Should I say that a literalist reading of the Bible was folly? Should I say that Mr. Keyes, who is a Roman Catholic, should ignore the teachings of the pope?

Unwilling to go there, I answered with what has come to be the typically liberal response in such debates—namely, I said that we live in a pluralistic society, that I can't impose my own religious views on another, that I was running to be the US senator of Illinois and not the minister of Illinois.

But Mr. Keyes's implicit accusation that I was not a true Christian nagged at me, and I was also aware that my answer did not adequately address the role my faith has in guiding my own values and my own beliefs.

Now, my dilemma was by no means unique. In a way, it reflected the broader debate we've been having in this country for the last thirty years over the role of religion in politics.

For some time now, there has been plenty of talk among pundits and pollsters that the political divide in this country has fallen sharply along religious lines. Indeed, the single biggest gap in party affiliation among white Americans today is not between men and women, or those who reside in so-called red states and those who reside in blue, but between those who attend church regularly and those who don't.

Conservative leaders have been all too happy to exploit this gap, consistently reminding evangelical Christians that Democrats disrespect their values and dislike their church, while suggesting to the rest of the country that religious Americans care only about issues like abortion and gay marriage; school prayer and intelligent design.

Democrats, for the most part, have taken the bait. At best, we may try to avoid the conversation about religious values altogether, fearful of offending anyone and claiming that—regardless of our personal beliefs—constitutional principles tie our hands. At worst, there are some liberals who dismiss religion in the public square as inherently irrational or intolerant, insisting on a caricature of religious Americans that paints them as fanatical, or thinking that the very word *Christian* describes one's political opponents, not people of faith.

Now, such strategies of avoidance may work for progressives when our opponent is Alan Keyes. But over the long haul, I think we make a mistake when we fail to acknowledge the power of faith in people's lives—in the lives of the American people—and I think it's time that we join a serious debate about how to reconcile faith with our modern, pluralistic democracy.

And if we're going to do that, then we first need to understand that Americans are a religious people. Ninety percent of us believe in God, 70 percent affiliate themselves with an organized religion, 38 percent call themselves committed Christians, and substantially more people in America believe in angels than they do in evolution.

This religious tendency is not simply the result of successful marketing by skilled preachers or the draw of popular megachurches. In fact, it speaks to a hunger that's deeper than that—a hunger that goes beyond any particular issue or cause.

Each day, it seems, thousands of Americans are going about their daily rounds—dropping off the kids at school, driving to the office, flying to a business meeting, shopping at the mall, trying to stay on their diets—and they're coming to the realization that something is missing. They are deciding that their work, their possessions, their diversions, their sheer busyness is not enough.

They want a sense of purpose, a narrative arc to their lives. They're looking to relieve a chronic loneliness, a feeling supported by a recent study that shows Americans have fewer close friends and confidants than ever before. And so they need an assurance that somebody out there cares about them, is listening to them—that they are not just destined to travel down that long highway toward nothingness.

And I speak with some experience on this matter. I was not raised in a particularly religious household, as undoubtedly many in the audience were. My father, who returned to Kenya when I was just two, was born Muslim but as an adult became an atheist. My mother, whose parents were nonpracticing Baptists and Methodists, was probably one of the most spiritual and kindest people I've ever known but grew up with a healthy skepticism of organized religion herself. As a consequence, so did I.

It wasn't until after college, when I went to Chicago to work as a community organizer for a group of Christian churches, that I confronted my own spiritual dilemma.

I was working with churches, and the Christians who I worked with recognized themselves in me. They saw that I knew their Book and that I shared their values and sang their songs. But they sensed that a part of me remained removed, detached, that I was an observer in their midst.

And in time, I came to realize that something was missing as well—that without a vessel for my beliefs, without a commitment to a particular community of faith, at some level I would always remain apart, and alone.

And if it weren't for the particular attributes of the historically black church, I may have accepted this fate. But as the months passed in Chicago, I found myself drawn—not just to work with the church but to be in the church.

For one thing, I believed and still believe in the power of the African American religious tradition to spur social change, a power made real by some of the leaders here today. Because of its past, the black church understands in an intimate way the biblical call to feed the hungry and clothe the naked and challenge powers and principalities. And in its historical struggles for freedom and the rights of man, I was able to see faith as more than just a comfort to the weary or a hedge against death but rather as an active, palpable agent in the world. As a source of hope.

And perhaps it was out of this intimate knowledge of hardship—the grounding of faith in struggle—that the church offered me a second insight, one that I think is important to emphasize today.

Faith doesn't mean that you don't have doubts.

You need to come to church in the first place precisely because you are first of this world, not apart from it. You need to embrace

Christ precisely because you have sins to wash away—because you are human and need an ally in this difficult journey.

It was because of these newfound understandings that I was finally able to walk down the aisle of Trinity United Church of Christ on 95th Street in the south side of Chicago one day and affirm my Christian faith. It came about as a choice and not an epiphany. I didn't fall out in church. The questions I had didn't magically disappear. But kneeling beneath that cross on the south side, I felt that I heard God's spirit beckoning me. I submitted myself to his will and dedicated myself to discovering his truth.

That's a path that has been shared by millions upon millions of Americans—evangelicals, Catholics, Protestants, Jews, and Muslims alike—some since birth, others at certain turning points in their lives. It is not something they set apart from the rest of their beliefs and values. In fact, it is often what drives their beliefs and their values.

And that is why that, if we truly hope to speak to people where they're at—to communicate our hopes and values in a way that's relevant to their own—then as progressives, we cannot abandon the field of religious discourse.

Because when we ignore the debate about what it means to be a good Christian or Muslim or Jew, when we discuss religion only in the negative sense of where or how it should not be practiced rather than in the positive sense of what it tells us about our obligations toward one another, when we shy away from religious venues and religious broadcasts because we assume that we will be unwelcome—others will fill the vacuum, those with the most insular views of faith or those who cynically use religion to justify partisan ends.

In other words, if we don't reach out to evangelical Christians and other religious Americans and tell them what we stand for, then the Jerry Falwells and Pat Robertsons and Alan Keyeses will continue to hold sway.

More fundamentally, the discomfort of some progressives with any hint of religion has often prevented us from effectively addressing issues in moral terms. Some of the problem here is rhetorical—if we scrub language of all religious content, we forfeit the imagery and terminology through which millions of Americans understand both their personal morality and social justice. Imagine Lincoln's second inaugural address without reference to "the judgments of the Lord." Or King's "I Have a Dream" speech without references to "all of God's children." Their summoning of a higher truth helped inspire what had seemed impossible and move the nation to embrace a common destiny.

Our failure as progressives to tap into the moral underpinnings of the nation is not just rhetorical, though. Our fear of getting "preachy" may also lead us to discount the role that values and culture play in some of our most urgent social problems.

After all, the problems of poverty and racism, the uninsured and the unemployed, are not simply technical problems in search of the perfect ten-point plan. They are rooted in both societal indifference and individual callousness—in the imperfections of man.

Solving these problems will require changes in government policy, but it will also require changes in hearts and a change in minds. I believe in keeping guns out of our inner cities and that our leaders must say so in the face of the gun manufacturers' lobby, but I also believe that when a gangbanger shoots indiscriminately into a crowd because he feels somebody disrespected him, we've got a moral problem. There's a hole in that young man's heart—a hole that the government alone cannot fix.

I believe in vigorous enforcement of our nondiscrimination laws. But I also believe that a transformation of conscience and a genuine commitment to diversity on the part of the nation's CEOs could bring about quicker results than a battalion of lawyers. They have more lawyers than us anyway.

I think that we should put more of our tax dollars into educating poor girls and boys. I think that the work that Marian Wright Edelman has done all her life is absolutely how we should prioritize our resources in the wealthiest nation on earth. I also think that we should give them the information about contraception that can prevent unwanted pregnancies, lower abortion rates, and help assure that every child is loved and cherished.

But, you know, my Bible tells me that if we train a child in the way he should go, when he is old he will not turn from it. So I think faith and guidance can help fortify a young woman's sense of self, a young man's sense of responsibility, and a sense of reverence that all young people should have for the act of sexual intimacy.

I am not suggesting that every progressive suddenly latch on to religious terminology—that can be dangerous. Nothing is more transparent than inauthentic expressions of faith. As Jim has mentioned, some politicians come and clap—off rhythm—to the choir. We don't need that.

In fact, because I do not believe that religious people have a monopoly on morality, I would rather have someone who is grounded in morality and ethics, and who is also secular, affirm their morality and ethics and values without pretending that they're something they're not. They don't need to do that. None of us need to do that.

But what I am suggesting is this: secularists are wrong when they ask believers to leave their religion at the door before entering into the public square. Frederick Douglass, Abraham Lincoln, William Jennings Bryan, Dorothy Day, Martin Luther King—indeed, the majority of great reformers in American history—were not only motivated by faith but repeatedly used religious language to argue for their cause. So to say that men and women should not inject their "personal morality" into public policy debates is a practical absurdity. Our law is by definition a codification of morality, much of it grounded in the Judeo-Christian tradition.

Moreover, if we progressives shed some of these biases, we might recognize some overlapping values that both religious and secular people share when it comes to the moral and material direction of our country. We might recognize that the call to sacrifice on behalf of the next generation, the need to think in terms of "thou" and not just "I," resonates in religious congregations all across the country. And we might realize that we have the ability to reach out to the evangelical community and engage millions of religious Americans in the larger project of American renewal.

Some of this is already beginning to happen. Pastors, friends of mine like Rick Warren and T. D. Jakes, are wielding their enormous influences to confront AIDS, Third World debt relief, and the genocide in Darfur. Religious thinkers and activists like our good friend Jim Wallis and Tony Campolo are lifting up the biblical injunction to help the poor as a means of mobilizing Christians against budget cuts to social programs and growing inequality.

And by the way, we need Christians on Capitol Hill, Jews on Capitol Hill, and Muslims on Capitol Hill talking about the estate tax. When you've got an estate tax debate that proposes a trillion dollars being taken out of social programs to go to a handful of folks who don't need and weren't even asking for it, you know that we need an injection of morality in our political debate.

Across the country, individual churches like my own and your own are sponsoring day care programs, building senior centers, helping ex-offenders reclaim their lives, and rebuilding our gulf coast in the aftermath of Hurricane Katrina.

So the question is, how do we build on these still-tentative partnerships between religious and secular people of goodwill? It's going to take more work, a lot more work than we've done so far. The tensions and the suspicions on each side of the religious divide will have to be squarely addressed. And each side will need to accept some ground rules for collaboration.

While I've already laid out some of the work that progressive leaders need to do, I want to talk a little bit about what conservative leaders need to do—some truths they need to acknowledge.

For one, they need to understand the critical role that the separation of church and state has played in preserving not only our democracy but the robustness of our religious practice. Folks tend to forget that during our founding, it wasn't the atheists or the civil libertarians who were the most effective champions of the First Amendment. It was the persecuted minorities, it was Baptists like John Leland who didn't want the established churches to impose their views on folks who were getting happy out in the fields and teaching the scripture to slaves. It was the forbearers of the evangelicals who were the most adamant about not mingling government with religious, because they did not want state-sponsored religion hindering their ability to practice their faith as they understood it.

Moreover, given the increasing diversity of America's population, the dangers of sectarianism have never been greater. Whatever we once were, we are no longer just a Christian nation; we are also a Jewish nation, a Muslim nation, a Buddhist nation, a Hindu nation, and a nation of nonbelievers.

And even if we did have only Christians in our midst, if we expelled every non-Christian from the United States of America, whose Christianity would we teach in the schools? Would we go with James Dobson's or Al Sharpton's? Which passages of scripture should guide our public policy? Should we go with Leviticus, which suggests slavery is okay and that eating shellfish is abomination? How about Deuteronomy, which suggests stoning your child if he strays from the faith? Or should we just stick to the Sermon on the Mount—a passage that is so radical that it's doubtful that our own Defense Department would survive its application? So before we get carried away, let's read our Bibles. Folks haven't been reading their Bibles.

This brings me to my second point. Democracy demands that the religiously motivated translate their concerns into universal, rather than religion-specific, values. It requires that their proposals be subject to argument and amenable to reason. I may be opposed to abortion for religious reasons, but if I seek to pass a law banning the practice, I cannot simply point to the teachings of my church or evoke God's will. I have to explain why abortion violates some principle that is accessible to people of all faiths, including those with no faith at all.

Now, this is going to be difficult for some who believe in the inerrancy of the Bible, as many evangelicals do. But in a pluralistic democracy, we have no choice. Politics depends on our ability to persuade each other of common aims based on a common reality. It involves the compromise, the art of what's possible. At some fundamental level, religion does not allow for compromise. It's the art of the impossible. If God has spoken, then followers are expected to live up to God's edicts, regardless of the consequences. To base one's life on such uncompromising commitments may be sublime, but to base our policy making on such commitments would be a dangerous thing. And if you doubt that, let me give you an example.

We all know the story of Abraham and Isaac. Abraham is ordered by God to offer up his only son, and without argument, he takes Isaac to the mountaintop, binds him to an altar, and raises his knife, prepared to act as God has commanded.

Of course, in the end God sends down an angel to intercede at the very last minute, and Abraham passes God's test of devotion.

But it's fair to say that if any of us leaving this church saw Abraham on a roof of a building raising his knife, we would, at the very least, call the police and expect the Department of Children and Family Services to take Isaac away from Abraham. We would do so because we do not hear what Abraham hears, do not see what Abraham sees, true as those experiences may be. So the best we can do is act in accordance with those things that we all see and that we all hear, be it common laws or basic reason.

Finally, any reconciliation between faith and democratic pluralism requires some sense of proportion.

This goes for both sides.

Even those who claim the Bible's inerrancy make distinctions between scriptural edicts, sensing that some passages—the Ten Commandments, say, or a belief in Christ's divinity—are central to Christian faith, while others are more culturally specific and may be modified to accommodate modern life.

The American people intuitively understand this, which is why the majority of Catholics practice birth control and some of those opposed to gay marriage nevertheless are opposed to a constitutional amendment to ban it. Religious leadership need not accept such wisdom in counseling their flocks, but they should recognize this wisdom in their politics.

But a sense of proportion should also guide those who police the boundaries between church and state. Not every mention of God in public is a breach to the wall of separation—context matters. It is doubtful that children reciting the Pledge of Allegiance feel oppressed or brainwashed as a consequence of muttering the phrase "under God." I didn't. Having voluntary student prayer groups use school property to meet should not be a threat, any more than its use by the high school Republicans should threaten Democrats. And one can envision certain faith-based programs—targeting ex-offenders or substance abusers—that offer a uniquely powerful way of solving problems.

So we all have some work to do here. But I am hopeful that we can bridge the gaps that exist and overcome the prejudices each of us bring to this debate. And I have faith that millions of believing Americans want that to happen. No matter how religious they may or may not be, people are tired of seeing faith used as a tool of attack.

They don't want faith used to belittle or to divide. They're tired of hearing folks deliver more screed than sermon. Because in the end, that's not how they think about faith in their own lives.

So let me end with just one other interaction I had during my campaign. A few days after I won the Democratic nomination in my US Senate race, I received an email from a doctor at the University of Chicago Medical School that said the following: "Congratulations on your overwhelming and inspiring primary win. I was happy to vote for you, and I will tell you that I am seriously considering voting for you in the general election. I write to express my concerns that may, in the end, prevent me from supporting you." The doctor described himself as a Christian who understood his commitments to be "totalizing." His faith led him to a strong opposition to abortion and gay marriage, although he said that his faith also led him to question the idolatry of the free market and quick resort to militarism that seemed to characterize much of the Republican agenda.

But the reason the doctor was considering not voting for me was not simply my position on abortion. Rather, he had read an entry that my campaign had posted on my website which suggested that I would fight "right-wing ideologues who want to take away a woman's right to choose."

The doctor went on to write: "I sense that you have a strong sense of justice . . . and I also sense that you are a fair minded person with a high regard for reason. . . . Whatever your convictions, if you truly believe that those who oppose abortion are all ideologues driven by perverse desires to inflict suffering on women, then you, in my judgment, are not fair-minded. . . . You know that we enter times that are fraught with possibilities for good and for harm, times when we are struggling to make sense of a common polity in the context of plurality, when we are unsure of what grounds we have for making any claims that involve others. . . . I do not ask at this point that you oppose abortion, only that you speak about this issue in fair-minded words."

Fair-minded words.

So I looked at my website and found the offending words. In fairness to them, my staff had written them using standard Democratic boilerplate language to summarize my pro-choice position during the Democratic primary, at a time when some of my opponents were questioning my commitment to protect *Roe v. Wade*.

Rereading the doctor's letter, though, I felt a pang of shame. It is people like him who are looking for a deeper, fuller conversation about religion in this country. They may not change their positions, but they are willing to listen and learn from those who are willing to speak in fair-minded words, those who know of the central and awesome place that God holds in the lives of so many and who refuse to treat faith as simply another political issue with which to score points.

So I wrote back to the doctor, and I thanked him for his advice. The next day I circulated the email to my staff and changed the language on my website to state in clear but simple terms my pro-choice position. And that night, before I went to bed, I said a prayer of my own—a prayer that I might extend the same presumption of good faith to others that the doctor had extended to me.

And that night, before I went to bed, I said a prayer of my own. It's a prayer I think I share with a lot of Americans. A hope that we can live with one another in a way that reconciles the beliefs of each with the good of all. It's a prayer worth praying and a conversation worth having in this country in the months and years to come. Thank you.

# Acknowledgments

Even the author who does not enlist others in his work owes a great literary debt. The voice he hears in his mind as he writes may have first been fashioned by his mother the storyteller or perhaps the older sister who often read aloud. An exceptional teacher may have seen and summoned his gifts. There were likely a thousand other authors who stoked his inner fire. He is debtor to those who make his isolation possible, who champion his cause, and who offer the crucial bit of wisdom at just the right time.

I owe all such debts and many more because I do enlist others in my work. I recognize that I am better with them than alone. All literature, I believe, is in some way a collaboration.

Among those to whom I am debtor are the many fine minds and devoted souls who spoke with me about the themes in this book. Joshua DuBois, once a spiritual advisor to President Obama and head of the White House Office of Faith-Based and Neighborhood Partnerships, took time from his own consulting and literary work to talk to me about religion and presidential politics. Jim Wallis of Sojourners was as wise and measured as he always is when advising me. Russell Moore, president of the Southern Baptist Ethics and Religious Liberty Commission, offered learned and passionate perspective,

233

as did my friend Mark Beliles, author of *Doubting Thomas: The Religious Life and Legacy of Thomas Jefferson* and founder of the Providence Foundation.

Tom DeLay, friend and conservative wise man, spoke with me about faith, about Hillary Clinton, and about Republican challenges to come. Dr. Paul Kengor of Grove City College shares my passion for understanding religion in American culture and offered the fruit of his great learning. His book *God and Hillary Clinton: A Spiritual Life* was invaluable.

Dr. Joel Hunter has kindly spent much time on the phone with me in recent years. Though he is the senior pastor of a church of nearly twenty thousand, a spiritual advisor to President Obama, and a man who has endured nearly unbearable heartbreak in recent years, he has always been patient, always been generous, and always offered perspective I could not have obtained but through him. I owe him much, as does our country.

A man whose work I find essential is George Barna. The polls and research conducted by his firm, the Barna Group, provide clearer insight into the current state of American culture, the current state of the American church, and what makes effective leadership than anything else I read. He has been criticized and even vilified because he reports the truth without apology to those entrenched in ineffective and outdated convention. I think of him as a "statistical prophet" and am grateful for his contribution to this book and for his contribution to my thinking and leadership. Rage on, George.

I will always be grateful that David Aikman agreed to write the foreword for this book. His stellar academic career, two decades as journalist and station chief for *Newsweek*, and firsthand experience with numerous American presidents and politicians made him the perfect choice. Thank you, David.

Those who write professionally about religion in politics are few in number in our country, but some of the best helped me with this book. Paul Raushenbush, the Executive Editor of Global Spirituality and Religion for *Huffington Post* and former Dean of Religious Life at Princeton, was—as I have always found him to be—gracious, wise, and encouraging. Groundbreaking religion writer Cathleen Falsani stirred my thinking in not one but two lengthy interviews. Sarah Pulliam Bailey of the *Washington Post* helped me understand her challenges and those of the surprisingly small band of national religion reporters who labor in her field. Bob Smietana, former President of the Religion Newswriters Association and Senior News Editor of *Christianity Today*, was as eager to help and as hilarious as he has always been in the years I have known him. I am grateful for the work of each of these craftsmen.

I have written much about American Mormonism in recent years. My conclusions have been my own, but I have had brilliant mentors, many of them Mormons themselves who knew we would not always agree. Dr. Kathleen Flake of Vanderbilt University taught me well. Equally helpful were historian Glen Leonard of the Latter-Day Saints Church History Museum and the Mormon History Association; Michael Otterson, chief executive of LDS Public Relations; Dr. Paul Reeve of the University of Utah; and Dr. Boyd Peterson of Utah Valley University's Mormon Studies program. Among non-Mormons, the eminent Jan Shipps kindly spent time with me, as did David Campbell of Notre Dame, the brilliant Michael Quinn, and the always fascinating Mitch Horowitz.

I am grateful, also, for the skill and encouragement of the good people at Baker Books. They have made both this book and its author better.

My own team proved typically invaluable in this project. My executive assistant, Karen Montgomery, researched, edited, and repaired the damage done. Garry Senna manned the digital barricades always with a laugh or two along the way. Isaac Darnall deployed his skills on our behalf and I'm grateful. Phil Newman's expert research and analysis were critical to my conclusions. Dan Williamson, Daniel Marrs, and Mary Johansen also gave wise and learned input.

It is one of the great pleasures of my life to include my children in my work. Elizabeth has worked for our firm, assisted me in numerous projects, and shown herself a wise and meticulous editor. I hear her voice as I write. Jonathan was invaluable when I wrote *The Faith of George W. Bush* and has been encouraging during this project too. I see his face when I write. It would be enough to simply love my children. To admire them also is more than I could have dared to ask.

Finally, if an author finds an agent who extends him, challenges him, and helps him prosper, it is the greatest gift of his career. If he also finds a wife he loves above all others and who loves him in return, it is the answer to the longing of his soul. Should he find a friend who walks with him through all that life demands, he is fortunate beyond words. I have found all three in one woman. It is the grace of God. I love you, Beverly.

# Select Bibliography

Ahlstrom, Sidney. *A Religious History of the American People*. New Haven: Yale University Press, 1972.

Balmer, Randall. *God in the White House: A History*. New York: HarperCollins, 2009.

Barrett, Patricia. *Religious Liberty and the American Presidency*. New York: Herder & Herder, 1963.

Beliles, Mark, and Jerry Newcombe. *Doubting Thomas? The Religious Life and Legacy of Thomas Jefferson*. New York: Morgan James Publishing, 2015.

Brodie, Fawn M. *No Man Knows My History: The Life of Joseph Smith*. New York: Random House, 1945.

Bushman, Richard Lyman. *Joseph Smith: Rough Stone Rolling*. New York: Random House, 2007.

Church, Forrest. *The Separation of Church and State*. Boston: Beacon Press, 2004.

Dreisbach, Daniel L. *Thomas Jefferson and the Wall of Separation between Church and State*. New York: New York University Press, 2002.

Fox, Jonathan. *Political Secularism, Religion, and the State*. New York: Cambridge University Press, 2015.

Gilbert, Martin. *Churchill: A Life*. New York: Henry Holt and Company, 1991.

———. *In Search of Churchill*. London: HarperCollins, 1994.

Grant, George. *Grand Illusions: The Legacy of Planned Parenthood.* Franklin, TN: Adroit Press, 1988, 1992.

————. *Killer Angel: A Biography of Planned Parenthood's Margaret Sanger.* Franklin, TN: Standfast Books, 2014.

Green, John C. *The Faith Factor: How Religion Influences American Elections.* Westport, CT: Praeger Publishers, 2007.

Hitchens, Christopher. *Thomas Jefferson: Author of America.* New York: HarperCollins, 2005.

Kengor, Paul. *God and Hillary Clinton: A Spiritual Life.* New York: Harper-Collins, 2007.

Koch, Adrienne, and William Peden, eds. *The Life and Selected Writings of Thomas Jefferson.* New York: Random House, 1944.

Lambert, Frank. *Religion in American Politics.* Princeton, NJ: Princeton University Press, 2008.

Levy, Leonard. *The Establishment Clause: Religion and the First Amendment.* New York: MacMillan, 1986.

Mansfield, Stephen. *The Faith of Barack Obama.* Nashville: Thomas Nelson, 2008.

————. *The Faith of George W. Bush.* New York: Penguin, 2003.

————. *The Mormonization of America.* Nashville: Worthy Books, 2012.

Marannis, David. *First in His Class.* New York: Simon & Schuster, 1995.

McCollister, John C. *God and the Oval Office.* Nashville: Thomas Nelson, 2005.

McCullough, David. *Truman.* New York: Simon & Schuster, 1992.

McDonald, Forrest. *Novus Ordo Seclorum: The Intellectual Origins of the Constitution.* Lawrence: University of Kansas, 1985.

Meacham, Jon. *American Gospel: God, the Founding Fathers, and the Making of America.* New York: Random House, 2006.

Melendez, Albert J. *The Religious Factor in the 1960 Presidential Election.* Jefferson, NC: McFarland & Company, 2011.

Moore, Edmund A. *A Catholic Runs for President.* New York: Ronald Press, 1957.

Noll, Mark. *America's God: From Jonathan Edwards to Abraham Lincoln.* Oxford: Oxford University Press, 2002.

Schlesinger, Robert. *White House Ghosts: Presidents and Their Speechwriters.* New York: Simon & Schuster, 2008.

Sheehy, Gail. *Hillary's Choice*. New York: Random House, 1999.

Smith, Scott Gary. *Religion in the Oval Office*. New York: Oxford University Press, 2015.

Sorensen, Ted. *Kennedy*. New York: HarperCollins, 1965.

Wills, Garry. *Under God*. New York: Simon & Schuster, 1990.

Woodward, Bob. *The Choice*. New York: Simon & Schuster, 1996.

# Notes

**Prologue**

1. The White House Correspondents' Association, www.whca.net/dinner.htm; Emily Yahr, Soraya Nadia McDonald, Helena Andrews, Emily Heil, Roxanne Roberts Krissah Thompson, Jessica Contrera, and Manuel Rolg-Frania, "Complete Coverage of the 2015 White House Correspondents Dinner," *Washington Post*, April 26, 2015, www.washington post.com/news/reliable-source/wp/2015/04/25/white-house-correspondents-dinner-2015 -live-complete-coverage/.

2. "The Media, Religion, and the 2012 Campaign for President," Pew Research Center, December 14, 2012, www.journalism.org/2012/12/14/media-religion-and-2012-campaign -president/.

3. Ibid.

4. Ibid.

5. Bobby Ross Jr., "Another One Bites the Dust? New York Times Religion Writer Taking His Talents to Broadway," Get Religion, March 10, 2015, www.getreligion.org/getreligion /2015/3/10/godbeat-news-new-york-times-religion-writer-moving-to-broadway.

6. Rod Dreher, "Why Are Newspaper Religion Reporters Quitting?" *American Conservative*, September 14, 2013, www.theamericanconservative.com/dreher/why-are-newspaper -religion-reporters-quitting/.

7. Andrew Beaujon, "Three Religion Reporters Leave Dailies, but the Job Isn't Vanishing," *Poynter*, September 12, 2013, www.poynter.org/news/mediawire/223500/three-religion -reporters-leave-dailies-but-the-job-isnt-vanishing/.

**Introduction**

1. Comte is pronounced "KŎmt."

2. Nadieszda Kizenko, "Russia's Orthodox Awakening," *Foreign Affairs* 92, no. 5 (2013), www.foreignaffairs.com/articles/139936/nadieszda-kizenko/russias-orthodox-awakening.

3. John Micklethwait and Adrian Wooldridge, "God Still Isn't Dead: The Decline of Religion in America Has Been Predicted Again and Again," *Wall Street Journal*, April 7, 2009.

4. Jonathan Fox, *Political Secularism, Religion, and the State: A Time Series Analysis of Worldwide Data* (New York: Cambridge University Press, 2015), 18.

5. Ibid.

6. Frank Newport, "More Than 9 in 10 Americans Continue to Believe in God," Gallup, June 3, 2011, www.gallup.com/poll/147887/Americans-Continue-Believe-God.aspx?utm_source=continue%20to%20believe%20in%20god&utm_medium=search&utm_campaign=tiles.

7. G. K. Chesterton, *What I Saw in America* (London: Hodder & Stoughton Limited, 1922), 12.

8. William Bradford, *Of Plimoth Plantation* (New York: Alfred A. Knopf, 1997), 76. This is in an edition edited by Samuel Eliot Morison.

9. Letter to Dr. Benjamin Rush, September 23, 1800, in *The Life and Selected Writings of Thomas Jefferson*, ed. Adrienne Koch and William Peden (New York: Modern Library, 1944).

10. Tom Foreman, "When History Speaks: Lincoln's Three Lessons for an Obama Second Term," CNN, November 13, 2012, www.cnn.com/2012/11/12/politics/lincolns-lessons-for-obama/index.html.

11. Worthington C. Ford et al., *Journals of the Continental Congress, 1774–1789* (Washington, DC: Government Printing Office, 1904–37), 32:340. Northwest Ordinance, 1787. Article 3: "Religion, morality, and knowledge, being necessary to good government and the happiness of mankind, schools and the means of education shall forever be encouraged."

12. "U.S. Religious Knowledge Survey," Pew Research Center, September 28, 2010, www.pewforum.org/2010/09/28/u-s-religious-knowledge-survey/.

13. For more on Comte, see Mary Pickering, *Auguste Comte, Vol. 1: An Intellectual Biography* (New York: Cambridge University, 2006); Andrew Wernick, *Auguste Comte and the Religion of Humanity: The Post-Theistic Program of French Social Theory* (New York: Cambridge University Press, 2001).

14. Stephen Mansfield, *The Faith of George W. Bush* (Lake Mary, FL: Charisma House, 2003).

15. Stephen Mansfield, *The Faith of Barack Obama* (Nashville: Thomas Nelson, 2008), xxiii.

### Profile: Forty-Nine Truths about Religion in America

1. Frank Newport, "More Than 9 in 10 Americans Continue to Believe in God," Gallup, June 3, 2011, www.gallup.com/poll/147887/americans-continue-believe-god.aspx. Note: 2013 Rasmussen and Harris polls report 74% and 88%, respectively.

2. This statistic and those that follow, unless otherwise noted, are taken from "America's Changing Religious Landscape," Pew Research Center, May 12, 2015, www.pewforum.org/2015/05/12/americas-changing-religious-landscape/. Among US Christians, the Pew Forum lists Mormons as 1.6% of the population, Jehovah's Witnesses as 0.8%, and "other" as 0.4%.

3. "Marital Status by Religious Group (2014)," Pew Research Center, www.pewforum.org/religious-landscape-study/compare/marital-status/by/religious-tradition/.

4. "The Global Religious Landscape: Muslims," Pew Research Center, December 18, 2012, www.pewforum.org/2012/12/18/global-religious-landscape-muslim/.

5. "Age Distribution and Median Age of Religious Groups," Pew Research Center, May 7, 2015, www.pewforum.org/2015/05/12/chapter-3-demographic-profiles-of-religious-groups/pr_15-05-12_rls_chapter3-00/.

6. "Gender Composition by Religious Group (2014)," Pew Research Center, www.pewforum.org/religious-landscape-study/compare/gender-composition/by/religious-tradition/.

7. "State of the Bible 2015," American Bible Society, www.americanbible.org/uploads/content/State_of_the_Bible_2015_report.pdf.

8. Jeffrey M. Jones, "Atheists, Muslims See Most Bias as Presidential Candidates," Gallup, June 21, 2012, www.gallup.com/poll/155285/atheists-muslims-bias-presidential-candidates.aspx.

9. Frank Newport, "Bias against a Mormon Presidential Candidate Same as in 1967," Gallup, June 21, 2012, www.gallup.com/poll/155273/bias-against-mormon-presidential-candidate-1967.aspx.

10. Albert Mohler, "The Scandal of Biblical Illiteracy: It's Our Problem," ChristianHeadlines, www.christianheadlines.com/columnists/al-mohler/the-scandal-of-biblical-illiteracy-its-our-problem-1270946.html.

11. "Many Americans Say Other Faiths Can Lead to Eternal Life," Pew Research Center, December 18, 2008, www.pewforum.org/2008/12/18/many-americans-say-other-faiths-can-lead-to-eternal-life/.

12. Joy Overbeck, "Is Barack Obama a Christian?" *American Thinker*, March 14, 2015, www.americanthinker.com/articles/2015/03/is_barack_obama_a_christian.html.

13. "Fast Facts about American Religion," Hartford Institute for Religion Research, www.hartfordinstitute.org/research/fastfacts/fast_facts.html#numcong.

14. "Fast Facts about American Religion," Hartford Institute for Religion Research, hirr.hartsem.edu/research/fastfacts/fast_facts.html#sizecong.

15. Ibid.

16. Dr. Richard J. Krejcir, "Statistics and Reasons for Church Decline," ChurchLeadership, www.churchleadership.org/apps/articles/default.asp?articleid=42346&columnid=4545.

17. Ibid.

18. Ihsan Bagby, "The American Mosque 2011," CAIR, January 2012, www.cair.com/images/pdf/The-American-Mosque-2011-part-1.pdf.

19. Ibid.

20. Michael Lipka, "Muslims Expected to Surpass Jews as Second-Largest U.S. Religious Group," Pew Research Center, April 14, 2015, www.pewresearch.org/fact-tank/2015/04/14/muslims-expected-to-surpass-jews-as-second-largest-u-s-religious-group/.

## Chapter 1: Kennedy at Houston

1. Charles Lincoln, *The Constitutional History of New York* (Rochester, NY: the Lawyers Cooperative Publishing Company, 1906), 451.

2. John C. Jeffries Jr. and James E. Ryan, "A Political History of the Establishment Clause," *Michigan Law Review* 100 (November 1, 2001): 300.

3. John Y. Simon, ed., *The Papers of Ulysses S. Grant* (Carbondale: Southern Illinois University Press, 2003), 26:343.

4. Edmund Morris, *The Rise of Theodore Roosevelt* (New York: Random House, 2001), 284.

5. Michael W. McConnell, "Is There Still a 'Catholic Question' in America? Reflections on John F. Kennedy's Speech to the Houston Ministerial Association," *Notre Dame Law Review* 86, no. 4 (2011): 1640.

6. George Santayana, "The Alleged Catholic Danger," *New Republic* 5, no. 63 (January 15, 1916): 269.

7. Eleanor Roosevelt, *The Autobiography of Eleanor Roosevelt* (New York: Harper & Row, 1961), 148.

8. Edmund A. Moore, *A Catholic Runs for President* (New York: Ronald Press, 1957), 21.

9. Ibid., 146.

10. New York Herald Tribune, July 5, 1960. Quoted in Albert J. Melendez, *The Religious Factor in the 1960 Presidential Election: An Analysis of the Kennedy Victory Over Anti-Catholic Prejudice* (Jefferson, NC: McFarland & Company, 2011).

11. Quoted in Melendez, *Religious Factor,* 24.

12. Patricia Barrett, *Religious Liberty and the American Presidency: A Study in Church-State Relations* (New York: Herder & Herder, 1963), 9.

13. *Newsday*, September 8, 1960, 98. Quoted in Melendez, *Religious Factor.*

14. Quoted in James Michener, *Report of the County Chairman* (New York: Random House, 1961), 100.

15. Paul Blanshard, *American Freedom and Catholic Power*, 2nd ed. (Boston: Beacon Press, 1958), 347.

16. Ibid.

17. John T. McGreevy, *Catholicism and American Freedom: A History* (New York: W. W. Norton, 2003), 170.

18. George Gallup, "Kennedy Chance Hurt by Religion Factor," *L.A. Times*, May 7, 1959.

19. John Seigenthaler, interview with author, Nashville, Tennessee, 2012.

20. Shaun A. Casey, *The Making of a Catholic President: Kennedy vs. Nixon 1960* (New York: Oxford University Press, 2009), 200.

21. *New York Times*, September 4, 1960, 48.

22. Barrett, *Religious Liberty and the American Presidency*, 25.

23. "On Questioning Catholic Candidates," *America*, March 7, 1959.

24. Philip Hannan, Nancy Collins, and Peter Finney Jr., *The Archbishop Wore Combat Boots—From Combat to Camelot to Katrina: A Memoir of an Extraordinary Life* (Huntington, IN: Our Sunday Visitor, 2010), 24.

25. Ibid., 206.

26. Quoted in Garry Wills, *Bare Ruined Choirs: Doubt, Prophecy, and Radical Religion* (New York: Doubleday, 1972), 80–81.

27. Interview with author, Camp Victory, Iraq, December 29, 2005.

28. "Election 2008: 43% Would Never Vote for Mormon Candidate," *Rasmussen Reports*, November 20, 2006, www.rasmussenreports.com/public_content/politics/top_stories/election_2008_43_would_never_vote_for_mormon_candidate.

29. "How the Public Perceives Romney, Mormons," Pew Research Center, December 4, 2007, www.pewforum.org/2007/12/04/how-the-public-perceives-romney-mormons/.

## Chapter 2: Test of the Fathers

1. T. S. Eliot, "Little Gidding," in *Four Quartets* (San Diego: Harcourt, 1943), v.

2. Page Smith, *The Shaping of America* (New York: McGraw-Hill, 1980), 3:38.

3. Ibid., 24.

4. Julian P. Boyd et al., eds., *The Papers of Thomas Jefferson* (Princeton, NJ: Princeton University Press, 1955), 11:93.

5. James Madison, *Notes of Debates in the Federal Convention of 1787* (New York: W. W. Norton, 1987), 209–10.

6. From the records of Jonathan Dayton, quoted in E. C. McGuire, *The Religious Opinions and Character of Washington* (New York: Harper & Brothers, 1836), 151.

7. Charles Warren, *The Making of the Constitution* (Boston: Little, Brown and Company, 1937), 250–51.

8. McGuire, *Religious Opinions and Character of Washington*, 152.

9. Benjamin Franklin Morris, *The Christian Life and Character of the Civil Institutions of the United States* (Philadelphia: George W. Childs, 1864), 253.

10. See M. E. Bradford, *A Worthy Company: Brief Lives of the Framers of the United States Constitution* (Plymouth, MA: Plymouth Rock Foundation, 1982).

11. Jacob E. Cooke, ed., *The Federalist* (Middletown, CT: Wesleyan University Press, 1961), 84:579.

12. Jonathan Elliot, ed., *The Debates in the Several State Conventions on the Adoption of the Federal Constitution* (Philadelphia: J. B. Lippincott & Company, 1941), 3:330.

13. Ibid., 4:330.

14. Ibid., 4:208.

15. Ibid., 5:446.

16. Ibid., 5:498.

17. *A Constitution or Frame of Government Agreed Upon by the Delegates of the People of the State of Massachusetts-Bay* (Boston: Benjamin Edes & Sons, 1780), 44.

18. "Constitution of Delaware," in *The Constitutions of the Several Independent States of America* (Boston: Norman and Bowen, 1785), 229.

19. Paul L. Ford, *Life of Jefferson*, vol. 9 (Cambridge: A. W. Elson and Co., 1904), 174.

20. Forrest Church, ed., *The Separation of Church and State: Writings on a Fundamental Freedom by America's Founders* (Boston: Beacon Press, 2004), 60.

21. George Washington to Tench Tighman, March 24, 1784, in *The Washington Papers: Basic Selections from the Public and Private Writings of George Washington*, ed. Saul Padover (Norwalk, CT: Easton Press, 1989).

22. Thomas Jefferson, *Autobiography of Thomas Jefferson* (New York: G. P. Putnam's Sons, 1914), 71.

23. John Locke, *A Letter Concerning Toleration* (Huttersfield, England: J. Brook, 1796), 62.

24. Joseph Story, *The Bench and Bar* (Chicago: Callaghan and Cockroft, 1870), 2:64.

25. Elliot, *Debates in the Several State Conventions on the Adoption of the Federal Constitution*, 4:199.

26. Ibid., 4:191–92.

27. Ibid., 4:208, emphasis added.

28. Ibid., 4:194, emphasis added.

29. Ibid., 4:198–99, emphasis added.

## Chapter 3: Noah's Wife Was Joan of Arc

1. "U.S. Religious Knowledge Survey," Pew Research Center, September 28, 2010, www.pewresearch.org/search/us+religious+knowledge+survey/.

2. Cathy Lynn Grossman, "Americans Get an 'F' in Religion," *USA Today*, March 14, 2007.

3. "History of Hate: Crimes against Sikhs Since 9/11," *Huffington Post*, August 7, 2012, www.huffingtonpost.com/2012/08/07/history-of-hate-crimes-against-sikhs-since-911_n_1751841.html.

4. Ibid.

5. Bill Mears, "Texas Man Executed for Post-9/11 Murder," *CNN*, July 20, 2011, www.cnn.com/2011/CRIME/07/20/texas.execution/.

6. Jarrett Murphy, "Hindu Beaten Because He's Muslim," *CBS News*, November 25, 2002, www.cbsnews.com/news/hindu-beaten-because-hes-muslim/.

7. Christian Avard, "Ambassador Claims Shortly before Invasion, Bush Didn't Know There Were Two Sects of Islam," *Raw Story*, August 4, 2006. Ambassador Galbraith has given varying accounts of Bush's words in his television appearances. See www.dailykos.com /story/2005/12/09/170606/-Bush-did-NOT-know-there-was-difference-between-Sunni-and -Shiite-Muslims-until-Jan-03#.

8. Jeff Stein, "Can You Tell a Sunni From a Shiite," *New York Times*, October 17, 2006, www.nytimes.com/2006/10/17/opinion/17stein.html?pagewanted=all.

9. Sarah Abruzzese, "FBI Depositions: Lack of Knowledge of Terrorism," *MSN*, December 4, 2006, www.nbcnews.com/id/16043255/ns/nbc_nightly_news_with_brian_williams -nbc_news_investigates/t/fbi-depositions-lack-terrorism-knowledge/#.VgLql7Rdpzc.

10. Avard, "Ambassador Claims."

11. A. B. C. Whipple, *To the Shores of Tripoli: The Birth of the U.S. Navy and Marines* (Annapolis, MD: Naval Institute Press, 1991), 38.

12. Florida Teacher Certification Examinations, "Test Information Guide for Social Science 6–12," 4th ed., 14, www.fl.nesinc.com/PDFs/SocSci6-12_TIG_4thEd_DOE040 115.pdf.

13. Joseph Laycock, "If We Don't Teach Religion in Schools, Americans Will Never Understand the Rest of the World," *Quartz*, April 15, 2015, qz.com/383348/if-we-dont -teach-religion-in-schools-us-kids-wont-understand-the-rest-of-the-world/.

14. Abington School District v. Schempp, 374 U.S. 203 (1963).

15. "Joint Statement of Current Law on Religion in the Public Schools," ACLU, www. aclu.org/joint-statement-current-law-religion-public-schools.

16. Astrid Dinter and Peter Schreiner, "Science and Religion in Schools: A German and Worldwide Perspective," *Metanexus*, March 6, 2008, www.metanexus.net/essay/science-and -religion-schools-german-and-worldwide-perspective; Matthew Bell, "Germany Seeks to Undermine Islamic Extremists with Religious Education," *PRI's the World*, February 26, 2015, www.pri.org/stories/2015-02-26/germany-seeks-undermine-islamic-extremists-religious -education.

17. "Putin Approves New Education Law," *Moscow Times*, December 31, 2012, www .themoscowtimes.com/news/article/putin-approves-new-education-law/473783.html; Stoyan Zaimov, "Russia Makes Religious Education Mandatory in Schools," *Christian Post Asia*, January 3, 2013, www.christianpost.com/news/russia-makes-religious-education-mandatory -in-schools-87634/.

18. "Supreme Court Rules Quebec Infringed on Loyola High School's Religious Freedom," *Canadian Press*, March 19, 2015, www.cp24.com/news/supreme-court-rules-that-quebec -infringed-on-private-school-s-religious-freedom-1.2287249.

19. Maria Liza Gatto, "Brazil: 49% of Schools Have Obligatory Religion Classes," *Pulsa Merica*, March 25, 2013, www.pulsamerica.co.uk/2013/03/25/brazil-49-of-schools-have -obligatory-religious-classes/.

20. John Kerry, "Remarks at the Launch of the Office of Faith-Based Community Initiatives," August 7, 2013, www.state.gov/secretary/remarks/2013/08/212781.htm.

21. Henry A. Kissinger, *The White House Years* (Boston: Little, Brown and Company, 1979), 54.

## Chapter 4: Three Words

1. The author was sitting one seat ahead of Mitt Romney on that Delta flight and over-heard these words.

2. Katy Glueck, "Mitt Romney Mormon Video Goes Viral," *Politico*, November 5, 2012, www.politico.com/news/stories/1112/83310.html.

3. Sarah Posner, "Romney and the End-Times," *Religion Dispatches*, November 2, 2012, http://religiondispatches.org/romney-and-the-end-times/.

4. Leigh Ann Caldwell, "Poll: Romney Receives Low Score for Convention Speech," *CBS News*, September 25, 2012, www.cbsnews.com/news/poll-romney-receives-low-score-for-convention-speech/.

5. Benjamin Knoll, "Did Anti-Mormonism Cost Mitt Romney the 2012 Election?" *Huffington Post*, December 18, 2013, www.huffingtonpost.com/benjamin-knoll/mitt-romney-mormon_b_4121217.html.

6. *Doctrine and Covenants*, 101:80—"And for this purpose have I established the Constitution of this land, by the hands of wise men who I raised up unto this very purpose."

7. Chris Lehmann, "Pennies from Heaven: How Mormon Economics Shape the GOP," *Harper's Magazine*, October 2011, harpers.org/archive/2011/10/pennies-from-heaven/.

8. T. George Harris, *Romney's Way* (Englewood Cliffs, NJ: Prentice-Hall, 1967), 44.

9. Kathryn Lofton, "Mormonism Cost Romney the Election (But It's Not What You Think)," *Religion Dispatches*, November 7, 2012, religiondispatches.org/mormonism-cost-romney-the-election-but-its-not-what-you-think/.

10. *Doctrine and Covenants*, 132:58–62.

11. *Journal of Discourses*, vol. 3, 266. "Plurality of Wives—The Free Agency of Man," remarks by President Brigham Young, delivered in the Bowery, Provo, July 14, 1855. jod.mrm.org/3/264.

12. Fawn Brodie, *No Man Knows My History: The Life of Joseph Smith* (New York: Random House, 1945), 174.

13. Eric Pace, *New York Times*, "Spencer Kimball, Mormon Chief, Dies," November 7, 1985, www.nytimes.com/1985/11/07/us/spencer-kimball-mormon-chief-dies.html.

14. Bruce R. McConkie, "All Are Alike unto God" (speech, Second Annual Church Educational System Religious Educator's Symposium, August 17–19, 1978).

15. John G. Turner, "Why Race Is Still a Problem for Mormons," *New York Times Sunday Review*, August 18, 2002.

16. "Interview: Kathleen Flake," PBS, April 26, 2006, www.pbs.org/mormons/interviews/flake.html#top.

17. D. Michael Quinn, *Early Mormonism and the Magic World View* (Salt Lake City: Signature Books, 1998), 59.

18. Richard Lyman Bushman, *Joseph Smith: Rough Stone Rolling* (New York: Alfred A. Knopf, 2005), 416.

19. William Saletan, "Divine Revision: How Mormons Will Come to Accept Homosexuality, "*Slate*, November 12, 2014, www.slate.com/articles/news_and_politics/frame_game/2014/11/mormons_will_accept_homosexuality_mormon_church_leaders_use_revelation_to.html.

20. Ibid.

## Chapter 5: Thomas Jefferson Was a None

1. John Pearson, *The Private Lives of Winston Churchill* (New York: Simon & Schuster, 1991), 128.

2. David McCullough, *Truman* (New York: Simon & Schuster, 1992), 463.

3. Ecclesiastes 1:9 NIV.

4. Steve McSwain, "'Nones' Are Now 'Dones': Is the Church Dying?" *Huffington Post,* January 15, 2015, www.huffingtonpost.com/steve-mcswain/nones-and-now-the-dones-t_b_6164112.html.

5. Hemant Mehta, "Where Did the Term 'Nones' Come From?" *Patheos,* January 11, 2013, www.patheos.com/blogs/friendlyatheist/2013/01/11/where-did-the-term-nones-come-from/.

6. "America's Changing Religious Landscape," Pew Research Center, May 12, 2015, www.pewforum.org/2015/05/12/americas-changing-religious-landscape/.

7. Liz Fields, "Quarter of Americans Convinced Sun Revolves around Earth, Survey Finds," *ABC News,* February 16, 2014, abcnews.go.com/US/quarter-americans-convinced-sun-revolves-earth-survey-finds/story?id=22542847; Denver Nicks, "A Quarter of Americans Want to Secede from the U.S.," *Time,* September 19, 2014, time.com/3404009/american-secession-scotland/; Emily Swanson, "Alien Poll Finds Half of Americans Think Extraterrestrial Life Exists," *Huffington Post,* June 21, 2013, www.huffingtonpost.com/2013/06/21/alien-poll_n_3473852.html.

8. Michael Lipka, "A Closer Look at America's Rapidly Growing Religious 'Nones,'" Pew Research Center, May 13, 2015, www.pewresearch.org/fact-tank/2015/05/13/a-closer-look-at-americas-rapidly-growing-religious-nones/.

9. Ibid.

10. Ed Stetzer, "The Rise of Evangelical 'Nones,'" *CNN,* June 12, 2015, www.cnn.com/2015/06/12/living/stetzer-christian-nones/.

11. Patricia U. Bonomi, *Under the Cope of Heaven: Religion, Society, and Politics in Colonial America* (New York: Oxford University Press, 1986), 220.

12. Rosalie Davis, ed., *Fredericksville Parish Vestry Book, 1742–1787* (Manchester, MO: self-published, 1978), 86–96; quote in Mark A. Beliles and Jerry Newcombe, *Doubting Thomas: The Religious Life and Legacy of Thomas Jefferson* (New York: Morgan James Publishing, 2015), 14.

13. "An Act for Establishing Religious Freedom," in *The Life and Selected Writings of Thomas Jefferson,* ed. Adrienne Koch and William Peden (New York: Modern Library, 1944), 313.

14. Ibid., 278.

15. Thomas Jefferson to John Page, May 4, 1786, ibid., 393.

16. Thomas Jefferson to Justin P. P. Derieux, July 25, 1788, founders.archives.gov/documents/Jefferson/01-13-02-0302.

17. Thomas Jefferson to George Washington, December 4, 1788, founders.archives.gov/documents/Jefferson/01-14-02-0111; Thomas Jefferson to W. Carmichael, December 25, 1788, founders.archives.gov/documents/Jefferson/01-14-02-0159.

18. Thomas Jefferson to James Madison, March 2, 1798, founders.archives.gov/documents/Madison/01-17-02-0061.

19. Thomas Jefferson to William Linn, July 31, 1791, founders.archives.gov/documents/Jefferson/01-20-02-0356.

20. Thomas Jefferson to Elbridge Gerry, March 29, 1801, founders.archives.gov/documents/Jefferson/01-33-02-0424.

21. Thomas Jefferson to Levi Lincoln, August 26, 1801, founders.archives.gov/documents/Jefferson/01-35-02-0111.

22. Thomas Jefferson to Danbury Baptist Association, January 1, 1802, www.loc.gov/loc/lcib/9806/danpre.html.

23. Thomas Jefferson to Levi Lincoln, August 26, 1801.

24. Thomas Jefferson to Charles Clay, founders.archives.gov/documents/Jefferson/03-08-02-0181.

25. Thomas Jefferson to Doctor Benjamin Rush, April 21, 1803, in *The Selected Religious Letters and Papers of Thomas Jefferson*, ed. Mark Beliles (Charlottesville, VA: America Publications, 2013), 109.

26. Thomas Jefferson to John Adams, August 22, 1813, founders.archives.gov/documents/Adams/99-02-02-6135.

27. Thomas Jefferson to George Logan, November 12, 1816. Dickinson W. Adams, *Jefferson's Extracts from the Gospels: The Philosophy of Jesus and the Life and Morals of Jesus* (Princeton, NJ: Princeton Press, 2014), 381.

28. Thomas Jefferson to William Short, October 19, 1822, founders.archives.gov/documents/Jefferson/98-01-02-3103.

29. Edgar Woods, *Albemarle County in Virginia* (Charlottesville, VA: Michie Company, 1901), 127; Luke 2:29 KJV.

30. William Harry Herndon and Jesse William Weik, *Herndon's Lincoln* (Chicago: Belford-Clarke, 1890), 439.

31. Ibid.

32. Emanuel Hertz, ed., *The Hidden Lincoln: From the Letters and Papers of William H. Herndon* (New York: Viking Press, 1938), 52.

33. Thomas Keneally, *Abraham Lincoln* (New York: Penguin, 2003), 29.

34. Don E. Fehrenbacher and Virginia Fehrenbacher, eds., *Recollected Words of Abraham Lincoln* (Stanford: Stanford University Press, 1996), 372–74.

35. Roy P. Basler, Marin Dolores Pratt, and Lloyd A. Dunlap, eds., *The Collected Works of Abraham Lincoln* (New Brunswick, NJ: Rutgers University Press, 1953), 4:192.

36. Ibid., 4:198–99.

37. Ibid., 4:205.

38. Ibid., 4:220–221.

39. Abraham Lincoln, *The Collected Works of Abraham Lincoln* (Rockville, MD: Wildside Press, 2008), 271.

40. Ta–Nehisi Coates, "I Claim Not to Have Controlled Events," *The Atlantic*, July 28, 2011.

41. Douglas L. Wilson, *Lincoln's Sword: The Presidency and the Power of Words* (New York: Vintage Books, 2007), 272.

42. Carl Sandburg, *Abraham Lincoln: The Prairie Years and the War Years* (New York: Harcourt Brace and Company, 1954), 665.

43. F. B. Carpenter, *Six Months at the White House with Abraham Lincoln* (Lincoln: University of Nebraska Press, 1995), 90.

44. McCullough, *Truman*, 463.

**Profile: Milestones in American Religion and Politics**

1. George Mason, Declaration of Rights, 1776, Personal Papers Collection, Library of Virginia, Richmond, Virginia.

2. Jared Sparks, ed., *The Writings of George Washington* (Boston: American Stationer's Company, 1837).

**Chapter 6: A Faith to Shape Her Politics**

1. Burns Strider, "'Grace Notes': The Quiet Unshakable Faith of Hillary Clinton," *Religion News Service*, April 8, 2015.

2. Cathy Lynn Grossman, "5 Faith Facts about Hillary Clinton, Social Gospel Methodist to the Core," *The Washington Post*, April 10, 2015.

3. John Pollock, *George Whitefield and the Great Awakening* (Herts, England: Lion Publishing, 1972), 82.

4. Gail Sheehy, *Hillary's Choice* (New York: Random House, 1999), 22–23.

5. David Maraniss, *First in His Class: A Biography of Bill Clinton* (New York: Simon & Schuster, 2005), 250.

6. Hillary Rodham Clinton, *It Takes a Village* (New York: Simon & Schuster, 1996), 171.

7. Norman King, *Hillary: Her True Story* (New York: Birch Lane Press, 1993), 8.

8. Paul Kengor, *God and Hillary Clinton: A Spiritual Life* (New York: HarperCollins, 2007), 16.

9. Charles Kenney, "Hillary: The Wellesley Years," *Boston Globe*, January 12, 1993.

10. Kengor, *God and Hillary Clinton*, 16.

11. Maraniss, *First in His Class*, 432–33. John Wesley never served in Parliament. Mrs. Clinton must have confused him with William Wilberforce.

12. Ibid., 433.

13. Kenneth L. Woodward, "Soulful Matters," *Newsweek*, October 31, 1994, 22.

14. Ibid.

15. Bob Woodward, *The Choice* (New York: Simon & Schuster, 1996), 130–32.

16. Kengor, *God and Hillary Clinton*, 155.

17. Ibid.

18. Peggy Noonan, "Farewell," *Wall Street Journal*, January 19, 2001. www.peggynoonan.com/132/.

19. Michael Luo, "Faith Intertwines with Political Life for Clinton," *New York Times*, July 7, 2007, www.nytimes.com/2007/07/07/us/politics/07clinton.html?pagewanted=all &_r=0.

20. "GOP Crashes Democratic Party," *Columbia Daily Tribune*, November 6, 2004, archive.columbiatribune.com/2004/nov/20041106news011.asp.

21. Raymond Hernandez and Patrick D. Healy, "The Evolution of Hillary Clinton," *New York Times*, July 13, 2005, www.nytimes.com/2005/07/13/nyregion/the-evolution-of -hillary-clinton.html.

22. Ibid.

23. Kengor, *God and Hillary Clinton*, 210.

24. Rebekah Metzler, "Hillary Clinton Supports Gay Marriage," *U.S. News and World Report*, March 18, 2013, www.usnews.com/news/articles/2013/03/18/hillary-clinton-supports -gay-marriage.

25. Michael McAuliff and Helen Kennedy, "Hil Has a Holy Cow over Immigrant Bill," *New York Daily News*, March 23, 2006, www.nydailynews.com/archives/news/hil-holy -immig-bill-article-1.576307.

26. David R. Guarino, "Hill at Tufts: Use the Bible to Guide Poverty Policy," *Boston Herald*, November 11, 2004.

27. Clair G. Osborne, *The Unique Voice of Hillary Rodham Clinton: A Portrait in Her Own Words* (New York: Avon Books, 1997), 88.

28. Mark Hensch, "Clinton: 'Deep-seated' Beliefs Block Abortion Access," *The Hill*, April 24, 2015, thehill.com/blogs/ballot-box/239974-clinton-deep-seated-beliefs-block-ab ortion-access.

29. Jesse Byrnes, "Hillary Clinton Defends Planned Parenthood amid Video Controversy," *The Hill*, July 23, 2015, http://thehill.com/blogs/ballot-box/presidential-races/249033-hillary-clinton-defends-planned-parenthood-amid-video.

## Chapter 7: The Narrative of Faith

1. Barack Obama, *The Audacity of Hope* (New York: Random House, 2006), 208.

2. George W. Bush, *A Charge to Keep: My Journey to the White House* (New York: Perennial, 2001), 136.

3. Ibid.

4. This account of the meeting between Bush and Blessitt was taken from Arthur Blessitt's website (www.blessitt.com) and was corroborated and further developed by the author's interviews with Blessitt on June 30, 2003, and with Jim Sale on June 17, 2003.

5. "The Day I Prayed with George W. Bush to Receive Jesus!" www.blessitt.com/Inspiration_Witness/PrayingWithGeorgeWBush/Praying_With_Bush_Page2.html.

6. Sarah Palin, *Going Rogue* (New York: HarperCollins, 2009), 22.

7. Peter Flaherty and Timothy Flaherty, *The First Lady* (Lafayette, LA: Vital Issues Press, 1996), 20–21.

8. George W. Bush, "Remarks at the National Day of Prayer and Remembrance," *Washington Post*, September 14, 2001, www.washingtonpost.com/wp-srv/nation/specials/attacked/transcripts/bushtext_091401.html.

9. Winston S. Churchill, *My Early Life* (New York: Charles Scribner's Sons, 1930), 28.

10. John Pearson, *The Private Lives of Winston Churchill* (New York: Simon & Schuster, 1991), 20.

11. Winston S. Churchill, *The Second World War: The Gathering Storm* (Boston: Houghton Mifflin Company, 1948), 667.

12. William Manchester, *The Last Lion: Winston Spencer Churchill, Visions of Glory, 1874–1932* (Boston: Little, Brown and Company, 1983), 25.

13. William Shakespeare, *Julius Caesar*, Act IV, Scene iii.

14. Charles Cecil Wall, *George Washington: Citizen-Soldier* (Charlottesville: University Press of Virginia, 1980), 146.

15. Ibid.

16. Elizabeth Keckley, *Behind the Scenes; or, Thirty Years a Slave and Four Years in the White House* (New York: G. W. Carleton, 1868), 228–29; confirmed in William Harry Herndon and Jesse William Weik, *Herndon's Lincoln* (Chicago: Belford-Clarke, 1890), 135.

17. James Robison, interview with author, Dallas, Texas, May 28, 2003.

18. Ibid.

19. William Safire, *Lend Me Your Ears: Great Speeches in History* (New York: W. W. Norton, 1992), 894.

20. Ibid.

21. Obama, *Audacity of Hope*, 222.

22. Ibid., 224.

23. Carl Bridenbaugh, *Mitre and Sceptre, Transatlantic Faiths, Ideas, Personalities, and Politics* (London, England: Oxford University Press, 1962), 244.

24. F. B. Carpenter, *Six Months at the White House with Abraham Lincoln* (Lincoln: University of Nebraska Press, 1995), 117–19.

25. Peter Wallsten and Scott Wilson, "Obama Endorses Gay Marriage, Says Same-Sex Couples Should Have Right to Wed," *Washington Post*, May 9, 2012.

26. Quoted in R. E. McMaster, *Wealth for All: Religion, Politics, and War* (Whitefish, MT: A.N., Inc., 1982), 85.

27. Luke 4:18 NIV.

28. James H. Cone, *A Black Theology of Liberation: Twentieth Anniversary Edition* (New York: Orbis, 1986), 45–46.

29. Michelle May, "A Politics of Conscience," United Church of Christ, June 22, 2007, www.ucc.org/a-politics-of-conscience.

30. Marvin Olasky, "Compassionate Conservation," *Veritas: A Quarterly Journal of Public Policy in Texas* (Fall 2000): 7–8.

31. Tony Carnes, "A Presidential Hopeful's Progress," *Christianity Today*, October 2, 2000, 62.

32. Bush, *A Charge to Keep*, 6.

33. Adolf Hitler, *Mein Kampf* (New York: Houghton Mifflin, 1969), 60.

Stephen Mansfield is a *New York Times* bestselling author whose books about religion and American presidents include *The Faith of George W. Bush*, *The Faith of Barack Obama*, and *Lincoln's Battle with God*. He has also written a wide variety of other books such as *The Search for God and Guinness*, *Killing Jesus*, and *Mansfield's Book of Manly Men*. A popular speaker who also advises leaders worldwide, Mansfield lives in Nashville and Washington, DC, with his wife, Beverly, who is an award-winning songwriter and producer. To learn more, visit StephenMansfield.TV.

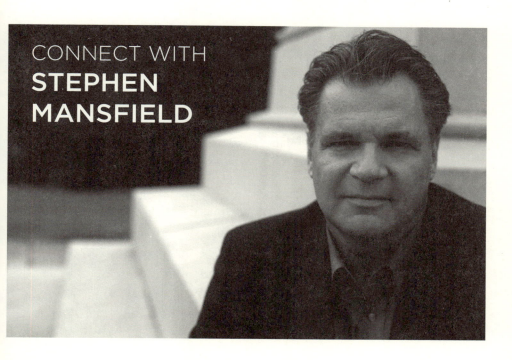

# LIKE THIS
# BOOK?
## Consider sharing it with others!

- Share or mention the book on your social media platforms. Use the hashtag **#AsktheQuestion**.

- Write a book review on your blog or on a retailer site.

- Pick up a copy for friends, family, or strangers! Anyone who you think would enjoy and be challenged by its message.

- Share this message on Twitter or Facebook: **"I loved #AsktheQuestion by @MansfieldWrites // StephenMansfield.TV @ReadBakerBooks"**

- Recommend this book for your church, workplace, book club, or class.

- Follow Baker Books on social media and tell us what you like.

 Facebook.com/ReadBakerBooks

 @ReadBakerBooks